THOMSON
———※———
COURSE TECHNOLOGY

Professional ■ Technical ■ Reference

Everyone
Should
DRAW

Les Pardew

Educational facilities, companies, and organizations interested in multiple copies or licensing of this book should contact the Publisher for quantity discount information. Training manuals, CD-ROMs, and portions of this book are also available individually or can be tailored for specific needs.

ISBN: 1-59863-256-6

Library of Congress Catalog Card Number: 2006923264

Printed in the United States of America

06 07 08 09 10 BU 10 9 8 7 6 5 4 3 2 1

Publisher and General Manager, Thomson Course Technology PTR:
Stacy L. Hiquet

Associate Director of Marketing:
Sarah O'Donnell

Manager of Editorial Services:
Heather Talbot

Marketing Manager:
Heather Hurley

Senior Acquisitions Editor:
Emi Smith

Marketing Coordinator:
Jordan Casey

Project Editor/Copy Editor:
Cathleen D. Snyder

PTR Editorial Services Coordinator:
Elizabeth Furbish

Interior Layout Tech:
Bill Hartman

Cover Designer:
Mike Tanamachi

Indexer:
Katherine Stimson

Proofreader:
Heather Urschel

THOMSON

COURSE TECHNOLOGY

Professional ■ Technical ■ Reference

™ Thomson Course Technology PTR, a division of Thomson Learning Inc.
25 Thomson Place ■ Boston, MA 02210 ■ http://www.courseptr.com

Acknowledgments

I want to acknowledge and thank all of the many people who have helped me to create this book. My deepest thanks go to my family and especially to my wife, who has put up with living with an artist and all of the ups and downs that brings. I also want to thank the many mentors who have taught me about art. They may never know how much they have influenced my life. I also want to thank my editors, Cathleen Snyder and Emi Smith, and publisher Stacy Hiquet, without whose help this book would have been impossible.

About the Author

Les Pardew is a video game and entertainment industry veteran with more than 22 years of entertainment industry experience. His work in the industry includes more than 120 video game titles, nine books, and numerous illustrations for magazines, books, and film. He began his career in film animation and later moved to video games, where he has found a permanent home. He currently serves as president of Alpine Studios, which he founded with Ross Wolfley in the fall of 2000.

Les is a prolific artist who loves to work on the computer and with traditional media. On the computer he is an accomplished 3D artist, creating and animating characters for many video games. In traditional media his first love is drawing, followed closely by oil painting. His favorite subject is people. He can often be seen drawing a portrait or designing a character for a game in his sketchbook.

Les loves to share himself with others, teaching business and art classes at the university level and authoring several books on art, animation, and game design.

Contents

3 Seeing Light 57

4 Developing Vision through Drawing 81

5 Gaining Perspective 97

6 Composition 125

Introduction

I have often thought that my experience as an artist has helped me to see the world in a very different way. It isn't that my world is different than anyone else's, but rather that the experience of my world is somehow richer and more meaningful because of my artistic training. The experience is richer because art training teaches one how to notice things that most people miss in their rush through life. The experience is more meaningful because art training teaches the meaning behind how and what we see in the world.

I approached this book with a great deal of excitement and anticipation. While I don't feel that I am the best artist in the world, I do feel that I have gained a greater appreciation of life and this world we live in through my art. It is the desire to share that appreciation with others that sparked the idea for this book. My hope is that by sharing what I know with others, I will be able to help them enrich their own lives.

In this book I attempt to show you how to experience life at a higher level through drawing. I chose drawing because it is the foundation of all art training. Drawing deals with artistic expression in its most basic and simplest form. It is also relatively inexpensive and available to almost everyone. All you need to draw are a pencil and a piece of paper.

Even though drawing is basic, the opportunity for artistic expression is limitless. With a few simple tools and a little training, even the most inexperienced artist can begin to create art that has depth and meaning.

I believe that anyone who wants to learn how to draw can do so unless there is some physical limitation that would bar him or her from doing so, such as blindness. Drawing is not a mystery. Anyone can draw and draw well if he puts time and effort into it. Some may say that they are not creative or that they can't draw because they tried when they were younger and failed. I don't agree with that; we all have creativity, and if you can write you can draw. In fact, writing *is* drawing.

Through drawing you will learn how to see things in a different way. Instead of just glossing over things, you will start to notice how things really look. You will learn how light enables vision. You will learn how shadow defines form. You will learn how depth is created. You will learn how to organize with a plan. You will learn patience. Most of all, you will learn how to open up a new world of expression that will bring you endless hours of enjoyment. How much better could this make your life? Do you want to see?

Well, pick up a pencil and a piece of paper, and let's get started. A new, more fulfilling world is waiting. It only takes the first step to begin your journey.

Artistic Vision

Not long ago I was discussing with a friend of mine his recent experiences in taking a drawing class at a local university. He commented on something I have often seen when teaching my own students drawing. He told me that he was amazed at all of the things he had never noticed before—things like the way light defines objects and how reflected light makes objects look like they have dimension. He spoke of colors and shading, of textures and motion, of composition and perspective. He commented that he really wasn't a very good artist, but that taking a drawing class was teaching him how to see. He stated, "I never knew how much I was missing in life until I took this art class."

My friend was gaining more in his drawing class than just the ability to draw. He was gaining something I call *artistic vision*. Artistic vision is the ability to see the world in a truer, clearer way. In other words, it is the ability to see and understand the world around us in a deeper, more profound manner. It enables the artist to see what most people miss.

Claesz, Pieter (1590-1661). Still Life with Drinking Glass and Silver Bowl. Bildarchiv Preussischer Kulturbesitz/Art Resource, NY

A trained artist who has learned to draw and paint realistically experiences life at a completely different level than does a person who has not had art training. The world becomes a rich and beautiful place full of wonder and excitement. Even mundane objects and places become interesting. Major art museums are filled with paintings of mundane scenes made interesting by the hands of great masters whose vision helped the rest of the world see wonder in the ordinary, such as this still-life painting by the Dutch artist Pieter Claesz.

This book is much more than a book about drawing. It is a book about seeing. It is a book that shows through artistic training how to see and experience the world through the eyes of the artist. It uses drawing as a way to unlock the beautiful from the ordinary, the interesting from the commonplace, the sublime from the mundane.

This book is designed not only to be a book about gaining artistic vision, but also to be a book about applying artistic vision to improve and enrich life. Because of that additional purpose, I will occasionally mention something from art that might be applied in a broader sense.

The Eye of the Artist

So what is it exactly that the artist sees? Why is it that the artist can experience the world on a higher level than most other people?

The answer to this question lies in two areas: seeing and understanding. First, an artist must learn to see. But seeing is only the beginning. The artist must also understand what he or she sees. For example, just seeing the shadow on a person's face as light splashes across it is one thing. Understanding how the shape of the shadow defines the structure of the face is something more. The artist not only sees the shadows on the face, but also understands the meaning of the shadows. This understanding gives the artist the ability to see shape and structure in everything. It gives the artist the ability to consciously recognize things like shape, structure, depth, solidity, and luminance.

Most people have a greater ability to see than they give themselves credit for. It isn't so much a matter of training a person to do something different as it is showing a person how to use what is already there. Let me give you an example.

Have you ever recognized a person's face, but not been able to place a name with the face? I want you to think about the complexities of facial recognition and the simplicities of a name. Why is it that our minds can distinguish the thousands of details associated with defining a person's face, yet the simple act of attaching a name to the person eludes us?

Most faces are very similar from the standpoint that there are two eyes, two ears, one nose, and one mouth. We all have cheeks on either side of our face and a chin just below our mouth. Given the similarities, it would seem that facial recognition would be a difficult task, yet we do it without even thinking about it. Many times it only takes one or two quick encounters for us to catalog a person's face in our memory.

Take a look at this figure. Don't spend a lot of time looking; just take a quick look and then turn the page.

©*Richard Polak, http://www.environment-textures.com*

©Richard Polak, http://www.environment-textures.com

Now that you have seen the pictures, can you pick out the person and the object from the pictures here without looking back at the previous picture?

For most people it is much easier to pick out the person than the object. Why is this?

From a very young age, a child learns the importance of recognizing people. The child puts a priority on learning how to find mother and father among a crowd of people. This skill of facial recognition is reinforced as the child grows older because there are more faces to recognize and more reasons to recognize them. The child learns to catalog the faces of family and friends. Recognizing people is emotionally important to the child. As time goes by, the process of facial recognition becomes so ingrained in the child's mind that it happens without conscious thought.

If the majority of us have such an ingrained ability to recognize a person's face, why are we all not portrait artists? Shouldn't it be relatively easy to take something as important as the face of a loved one and put it down on paper?

After years of teaching art, I have found that for most beginning art students there is almost a fear of drawing a person. Many young artists tell me that they are good at drawing almost anything except people. I believe that the reason many artists struggle with drawing people is the same reason we are so good at recognizing people. We place more importance on people than we do on other things in our world. We are so familiar with people that we instinctively know when something is not right.

If I draw a tree and I don't get one of the branches in the right place, most people will never even notice as long as the branch is in the general area that it should be. If, on the other hand, I move a person's eye even a few millimeters, almost everyone will notice, like in the picture shown here. This added pressure to draw a person's face correctly places a heavy burden on the shoulders of the beginning artist.

Successful portrait artists have learned to take their subconscious ability to recognize faces and bring it to conscious thought. In other words, the portrait artist is trained to recognize the differences in faces and the reasons why one face looks different than another. This ability enables the artist to then draw a picture that resembles the subject of the portrait. The portrait artist has learned to unlock the ability to see and understand, and has combined that with an ability to express these things.

Learning to see and understand can go far beyond art. Most misconceptions are a result of not seeing something correctly or not understanding. Artists have to look for truth in what they see; otherwise, they will be unable to draw the subject of the picture accurately. The artist sees more because he knows that he can't draw a subject if he doesn't understand it. Sometimes this takes a lot of time, but the results are worth it. Wouldn't it be great if everyone had to learn to really search for the truth in what they see?

The Artistic Process

A good way to begin to see and understand is to learn the artistic process—in other words, the process an artist goes through to create a picture. Not every artist goes through the same process, but there are some basic concepts that every artist deals with when creating art based on something seen in the real world.

The artistic process goes something like this:

► **Select**
► **Frame**
► **Arrange**
► **Express**

Some of these steps might happen rapidly or they might happen out of order, but they are almost always present when creating any realistic picture. Even when an artist is creating something from imagination, many of these steps are still present. Let's look at each one and see how it works.

Selecting

Something that I commonly do when training artists to draw is arrange the class in a circle and place a number of objects on a table in the center of the room. The objects can be anything. Usually I just find a number of things lying around the classroom and pile them haphazardly on the table. I then ask the students to find something interesting to draw. I challenge them to walk around the table and make several quick drawings until they find something they like.

The purpose of the exercise is to teach the class to put some effort into selecting their subjects. I am not as worried about the students drawing the objects accurately as I am about them finding something interesting to draw. Take a look at the picture here and try drawing something from it.

At first the students wander around the classroom somewhat aimlessly. Some might find interesting subjects quickly, but most have no idea what they are looking for. It is as if they are asking me, "What makes something interesting?" This very question is the heart of what I am looking for from them.

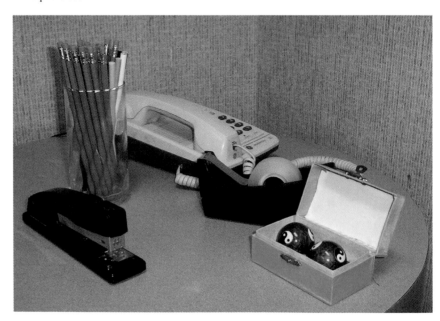

What makes something interesting? Is it the object itself? Is there something about the object that has meaning, like a picture of a child has meaning to his or her mother? Is there something symbolic? Is there something about the scene or object that symbolizes something more? Is there something beautiful? Is there something that stirs the feelings of admiration? Is there something powerful? Is there something about the contemplated picture that invokes a feeling of awe? Is there something funny? Does the scene you are about to draw have something hilarious in it? Is there something profound? Is there something that causes deep thinking?

Finding something interesting to draw is the first challenge an artist undertakes when lifting a pencil to a blank sheet of paper. Some artists might doodle a bit or play with some shapes or lines, but even that is searching for something interesting.

Artists tend to look at things a little differently than other people. I remember walking with a friend in a foreign country. While walking by a tree, I found it to have an interesting trunk. I stopped to take a picture. My friend was surprised because there I was, in a foreign country, taking a picture of a tree.

"We have trees in America," he commented. With all of the many different things around us that were exotic and new, why was I interested in a tree trunk?

It wasn't that I had no interest in the other things. They were all interesting to me. It was just that that tree trunk was unique. I had never seen a trunk like that before, and I wanted to record it so I could remember it for one of my drawings. I liked the way the wood turned in on itself.

Sometimes the interesting thing about a scene or object might be the lighting, the pattern the object makes, or any number of other elements that have nothing to do with the scene itself. To the artist, painting a tree might have very little to do with the tree and more to do with the way the branches twist and turn, reaching upward to the sky. A picture of a person might have little to do with the person and a lot to do with the person's actions or something the person is wearing. Often the challenge to the artist is finding what most people miss.

Take a few minutes right now and look around where you are sitting. I found this picture just outside of my office. See if you can identify something interesting to draw. Use some of the questions I posed earlier to help guide you in your search. Even if you can't come up with something right away, work at it for a while. Don't worry if you think others might not be interested in what you find. If it is interesting to you, that is all that matters right now.

Have you ever watched young children at the zoo or exploring a city park? Everything is new and exciting. Their eyes are filled with wonder. They run from one exciting thing to the next. Do you remember those days in your own life, or are they gone now? Does life still hold wonder? If not, where has that wonder gone?

I often find that artists tend to look much younger than they really are. For some reason the years don't seem to touch them the same way they do for most people. While the cares of the world can beat down on all of us, the true artist seems to find joy and wonder in even the smallest of things. I believe that having interest in life is a powerful force for contentment. Even though artists tend to be poor and often struggle financially, their lives are full and rich because the wonder of this world hasn't escaped them yet.

Today I awoke to the first snow of the season. As the morning sky cleared, ragged clouds ranged across the sky, clinging to the mountains with their chill embrace. The air that had been hazy for the last several weeks was now crisp and clear. From where I stood above the valley, I could see for miles the earth and lake below, covered with a blanket of pristine white. What a beautiful scene. How my life was enriched today by experiencing the view!

Life becomes boring because we lose interest in it. If your life has become dull and boring, it probably isn't because the world has become dull, but because you have stopped looking for all that is wonderful in it. Try looking at the world as an artist. Try drawing random things in your life and see whether they become more intriguing. You might surprise yourself by actually enjoying the small, common things once more.

Framing

Framing is the process of defining the boundaries of a picture. It is deciding what goes into a picture and what does not. It is deciding on a close-up of the subject or a distant view. Framing is the beginning step in determining what your drawing will become.

There is no place in art where framing is more critical than in photography. I remember hearing the story of the legendary nature photographer, Ansel Adams. He was to participate in a photography contest. The idea was to gather several photographers and have them take pictures of the surrounding area. It is said that unlike all of the other photographers, who were snapping photographs of everything they could find, Ansel spent his time just driving around the countryside. According to the story, he only took one picture. He found a location and waited late into the night. Then, when the moon crested the rise and washed the area with moonlight, he took his photograph. He won the competition.

Sometimes what doesn't go into a picture is as important as what does go into it. In the picture "The Wait," I wanted to tell the story of a wealthy, grasping king.

The old king sits on his throne, holding a bow representing the violence used to obtain his power. The jewels represent his wealth. He grasps the chair with frustration. The entire right side of the picture is empty. Although he has gained a kingdom, he has lost much in doing so. The right side of the painting represents the loneliness and emptiness of his existence. For this painting the empty right side was very important.

Framing Card

Artists will often create a framing card to help define the edges of a picture. A framing card is a small card with a rectangle or square hole cut in the middle. Artists use framing cards to block out surrounding detail and only look at what could be in a picture. It is like looking through the viewfinder of a camera, only without the camera. With a framing card you can quickly look at a scene and see what it would look like as a picture.

Let's try some experiments. Create a framing card. Don't worry if you have to put this book down while you create the card. I understand. I'll wait until you are finished with the card, then we can go on.

Do you have the card? Good. Take the card and hold it up to a scene. You can look at something in your house or apartment, or you can look at something outside. It doesn't really matter what you look at through your card; just find something or someone interesting. See whether you can frame the entire object or person in your framing card.

Now look at everything you can see through your card that is not part of the object or person. Notice the shapes formed by these picture elements. In this picture, I removed the flower so you can better see the surrounding shapes. Notice that there are a few petals from another flower in the lower-right corner. There are also a number of leaves that are only partially in the picture frame. The leaves run underneath the flower and form a random pattern of intersecting shapes.

A good artist will consider every element within the picture frame, and if something doesn't work, the artist will move or change the picture until it does. The petals in the lower-right might tend to draw attention away from the central flower. The artist can simply change that part of the picture and paint other leaves instead of the flower petals.

Now let's try something else. Bring the framing card closer to your eyes, so that you are framing the object or person as the central item in a larger picture. Here, I have framed the flower as only a part of the scene. Notice that while the flower is still dominant, other picture elements are competing for attention as well.

In this picture the central flower is offset by the more mature seedling flower on the lower-right side. This combination of young and old could make for an interesting theme for a drawing. I often find that by trying out different framing methods, I stumble upon ideas for drawing. See whether pulling back from your scene might give you an idea for a drawing.

Let's try this one more time. Instead of pulling back from the object or person in your framing card, try moving in a little closer. Here I framed the upper-left corner of the flower. Notice that changing the view to a close-up of the flower completely changes the nature of the picture. While we still know we are looking at a flower, the petals take on a more dominant role in the picture.

As you can see from these examples, framing can be a great tool for isolating and defining the picture area. Try using your framing card a little and see whether you can find some interesting things to draw.

Shapes

It is very common for us to identify the things we see in the world around us. In fact, much of our seeing involves identification. We see the world as separate identifiable parts. When you look through your framing card, do you see shapes or do you see objects, animals, and/or people? While this process of identification is useful in navigating life, it can sometimes impede your ability to see shapes in art.

If you are unfamiliar with artistic terms, you are probably asking yourself, "What is this guy talking about? What does he mean by shapes?"

Good question. I want to take just a moment to define shapes so you can better understand what I mean here.

A drawing is a two-dimensional representation inscribed by an artist. A drawing can represent a person, place, or thing, or it can be an idea. No matter what the drawing represents, it remains a two-dimensional image made up of shapes.

Shapes are elements in the drawing that are defined by edges. If you remember, earlier in this chapter I isolated the shape of a flower by painting it white. This made the shape of the flower more evident. It also helped us see the shapes behind the flower.

Take another look at those flower pictures. Can you see shapes within the flower? In this figure I have defined the shape of a single petal. Notice that the flower is made up of petals circling the center of the flower. Other than minor differences, each petal is similar to the other petals of the flower.

Even though the petals are similar in life, they are not similar in the picture. This is because many of the petals overlap each other. This is very important to understand. In a two-dimensional drawing of the flower, each petal has to be seen as it is. If a petal overlaps another petal, the shape of the overlapped petal changes. In this figure the isolated petal shape is very different because it is overlapped by surrounding petals.

Artists have to train themselves to view things as shapes because that is how the objects are defined on paper. Every element of the drawing is a shape. If you can teach yourself to see things in your drawing as shapes *and* as specific, identifiable things, you will be taking a big step in understanding how to design your drawings.

Shapes can be either positive or negative. Every picture is a combination of both positive and negative shapes. For example, the flower in the earlier examples is a positive shape. The area surrounding the flower is the negative shape. Without the negative shape there would be no positive shape. Let me try to be a little clearer. Imagine, for example, you are drawing a portrait of a person. The shape of the person's head is a positive shape. The area surrounding the head is the negative shape.

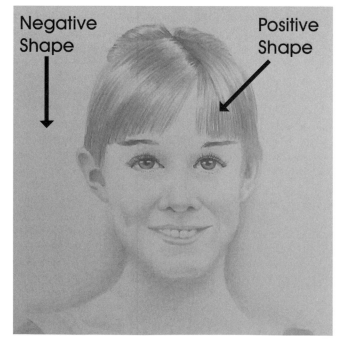

Negative Shape

Positive Shape

Here is another example. This figure shows a number of negative shapes. You should be very familiar with these shapes because you see them all the time. Do you know what these shapes are?

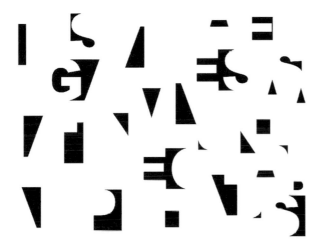

They are the negative shapes that surround letters in the English alphabet. If we organize the negative shapes into a specific order, you will see that they offset the positive shapes of the letters. In the following figure the negative shapes are organized so you can see that they are the shapes that define the words NEGATIVE SHAPES.

NEGATIVE
SHAPES

Take a look through your framing card and see whether you can see the negative shapes. Try drawing a few sketches by just outlining the shapes. As you begin to see shapes, you will expand your artistic perception.

Have you ever noticed that the way we perceive life depends a lot on how it is framed? In media, they call it *spin.* I believe the phrase is, "How can we spin this?" or "What kind of spin can we put on this?" We also talk about a frame of reference or a frame of mind as having an effect on how we see things.

I remember selling a picture of a seed pod. What was interesting about the sale of the picture is that the person buying the picture said to me that he liked the picture because he loved grey. I found this funny because there was no real grey in the picture. What the picture did have was a large grey mat surrounding it. Even though the picture had no grey, the buyer saw the picture as grey because of how it was framed.

For the artist, framing is creating a boundary. It is the process of isolating the picture from the rest of the world. The creation of the boundary helps the artist to define the picture. In life we also have boundaries that define who and what we are. These boundaries might be our jobs or they might be our families or any number of other things that define us. Boundaries are not bad things. No drawing is endless. Every drawing has to have a boundary or it lacks definition. Life without boundaries also lacks definition.

Sometimes we think that boundaries inhibit our freedom. I have found that in art just the opposite is true. Boundaries spark my creativity. Boundaries help me to better organize my picture. Boundaries help me to better define and express my art. I have also found that boundaries have the same effect on my life.

Arranging

Arranging a drawing is organizing the elements of the drawing to best express your goal. Artists often call it *composition* or *picture design*. The artist composes the drawing much the same way a musician composes a symphony, except where the musician's boundaries might be time, the artist's boundaries are the edges of the paper. The artist is responsible for everything that is within the frame of the picture.

Design Rules

Over the years some general rules for composing pictures have come into being to help artists better arrange their artwork. There are no hard rules in composition, only guidelines. With every rule there is an example of an artist successfully breaking that rule. Rules in picture composition are a little like grammar rules in the English language. They are guidelines that can be used to help the artist create more pleasing pictures. In Chapter 6, "Composition," we will take a detailed look at many of these rules.

Thumbnail Sketches

One of the best ways to arrange your drawings is to use thumbnail sketches. The term "thumbnail sketch" comes from the fact that these sketches are usually small. They are not as small as your thumbnail unless you have very big thumbs, but they are small—usually no more than one or two inches in any direction.

A thumbnail sketch is not a finished drawing; rather, it is a planning drawing. Thumbnails are used for planning finished drawings. An artist creates thumbnail sketches to explore ideas. In this figure I have four different thumbnail sketches on a single sheet of a sketchbook. You can see from the drawings that they are neither detailed nor accurate.

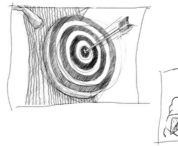

The idea of a thumbnail sketch is to quickly put down on paper your ideas for drawings. Beginning artists often get hung up on the fact that their drawings are not well-crafted. Don't worry about your drawing skill with thumbnails. You are just jotting down ideas. It's kind of like taking notes. The thumbnails are for you only, and you don't have to show them to anyone. Think of them as doodling with a format. Each thumbnail should be framed with a line to indicate the boundaries of the picture.

Try looking through your framing card and drawing some quick thumbnail sketches. Keep your drawing time to about a minute per thumbnail. This will force you to draw quickly. You might be surprised at what you come up with.

Once you get the hang of drawing quick thumbnail sketches, you can start working on rearranging your pictures. Suppose, for example, you see a person standing on the street. You want to draw the person, but you don't like the background. Maybe the person is standing in front of a wall or building, and you want to put him in an imaginary setting, such as a jungle or a beach. As an artist you are free to make those changes. In fact, you can make any change you want because artists are licensed to do that. It is called *artistic license*, and every artist—even a beginner—has one. That is one of the beautiful aspects of art. The artist has unlimited potential because art is a combination of the artist's experiences and imagination.

In this figure the three sketches are depictions of imaginary places and people. The sketches are larger and more detailed than the thumbnail sketches, but they are still not finished drawings.

Try drawing a few pictures completely or mostly from your imagination. Don't worry a lot about the drawing being good. Instead, concentrate more on getting your ideas on paper, even if they don't look exactly right. Remember, with a little practice you will get better at drawing and your pictures will improve.

Arranging a picture is really the process of organizing. In art, organization is important because it defines the relationships between elements in the drawing. The way a picture is organized can often determine whether the picture is just a drawing or a masterpiece.

In life, we also organize things. Many people use planners or other such tools to help them organize their days, weeks, and years. The organization of our life—or the lack thereof—can sometimes determine whether our life is a masterpiece or simply a drawing.

Wouldn't it be great if we could make some thumbnail sketches of our life before we had to live it? A thumbnail sketch forces the artist to concentrate on the overall effect of the many elements of the picture. Because the sketch is so small and done so quickly, the artist has to concentrate on the major elements of the picture and ignore the details. What if we could do the same thing in life? What if we could make a quick sketch of a segment of our life so we could see the major elements without the details? Wouldn't that help us plan our lives better? Wouldn't that help us place the major things in order so that then we could plan the details?

I think there are times in life when we need to pause and do a few thumbnail sketches. We need to take the time to see the major things, and then organize them so that when we are dealing with life's details, we do so with a plan for life's major elements.

Expressing

Expressing is the pure act of drawing. The two pictures at the top of the next page are sketches that try to express a mood. In some ways drawing is a performing art, similar to playing a musical instrument. It requires skill in execution. Like a musician who has to understand how to hold and use a bow on a violin, the artist has to understand how to hold and use a pencil. This might sound simple, and you might think you already know how to use a pencil. An artist, however, uses the pencil differently than most people learn in school. To talk about expression, first you need a foundation in the basics.

Understanding how to draw begins with understanding the tools of drawing. Drawing with the wrong tools can be frustrating, causing many people to give up before they even get started. Drawing becomes much easier once you start using the right tools in the right way.

Holding and Using the Pencil

One of the biggest problems beginning artists have is that they don't hold the pencil correctly for drawing. The problem is not so much that the artist holds the pencil incorrectly as it is that the artist needs to learn how to hold the pencil in different ways for different purposes. Most beginning artists hold the pencil for drawing the same way they hold it for writing.

Drawing is a very different process from writing. When a person writes, he is creating precise, small characters on a paper. Although this action is similar to drawing, in which precise detail is needed, it is very different from the action needed for blocking in a drawing or for achieving fine, smooth shading.

When a pencil is held in the writing position, beginning artists tend to tighten up and limit the movement of the pencil to the range of motion in the fingers. This is because the hand rests on the paper. The figure at the right shows the typical writing position of the hand.

In the initial stages of a drawing, freedom of movement is very important. Try holding the pencil similar to how you would hold a butter knife, as shown in this figure.

Let's do a little practicing. Find yourself some paper and a pencil. This picture is taken from a book Ross Wolfley and I created, called *The Animator's Reference Book* (Thomson Course Technology PTR, 2005). This book is a great artistic reference for the human body in a variety of actions. I want you to use the picture here to help you loosen the way you start a drawing.

Holding the pencil in the butter-knife position makes it almost impossible to draw using only finger movement. Instead, the whole arm is brought into play. If this is the first time you have ever drawn holding a pencil in the butter-knife position, it might feel a little awkward at first. Stay with it until you become comfortable. The long-term benefits from learning to hold your pencil in this position are immeasurable. It will allow you to draw with much more freedom than holding the pencil in the writing position will.

Prop up your drawing surface almost like it is on an easel. Take the pencil and hold it as you would a butter knife. I know this might feel a little awkward, but it will force you to draw with your arm rather than with your wrist. I will explain why it is better to draw with your arm in a moment; for now, just give it a try. Now quickly sketch the photo. Try to capture the essence of the movement in less than 60 seconds. Yes, this is speed drawing and it is good for you, so don't complain about the time limit. You're not doing a finished drawing. This is just an exercise. It's kind of like stretching before a long-distance race. You need to get loosened up.

This figure shows a sketch that I did. Your sketch should be similar, but it's okay if it is not exactly the same. I made this sketch in about 30 seconds, focusing only on trying to capture the feeling of movement. There probably isn't a single line in the drawing that is technically accurate with regard to the exact outline of the figure. In fact, most of the lines in this drawing follow the skeleton of the figure more than they do the outside shape.

For you to draw with the pencil in the butter-knife position, you have to move your arm, not your fingers. The human body is an organic yet mechanical construct. The muscles in our arms are like hydraulic pistons contracting and expanding to create movement. Unlike hydraulics, however, the placement of the muscles and the way they are attached to the bones of our skeleton is very organic. This is very important because it allows the body to move in fluid, non-mechanical ways. It is the attachment of the muscles and the shape of our bones that allow for grace of movement. Why is all of this important? It teaches you how to dance with your drawing.

Dancing with the Drawing

Dancing with the drawing means that you take advantage of the natural motions of the body to add expression to the drawing. By holding the pencil in the butter-knife position, you are better able to dance with the drawing. In other words, think of yourself as a dancer. Try to move your arm in graceful, smooth, flowing motions. It isn't that you are giving up control of your drawing; rather, you are gaining control by letting the natural rhythm of your body express itself in your drawings.

> **Hint**
>
> As you draw, hopefully you will notice that there is a main line of motion in each figure. The main line of motion is the foundation line of capturing the motion of the figure. To find the main line of motion, create a line from the head, following the spine down through one of the legs. Try drawing this line first and then attaching the rest of the body to the line. It will help you gain a feeling for motion.

Now try a couple more drawings. Here are two more photographs from *The Animator's Reference Book.* Try quickly sketching both photographs. Try to indicate as quickly as you can the basic motion captured in the photo. If you need to, draw them several times until you feel good about your creation. The idea here is not to create an accurate picture; rather, it is to indicate the essence of the figure.

Hint

The butter-knife position is great for starting a drawing, but it doesn't work too well for fine detail or delicate shading. The writing position is better for fine detail, but you will need to learn another way to hold the pencil for delicate shading.

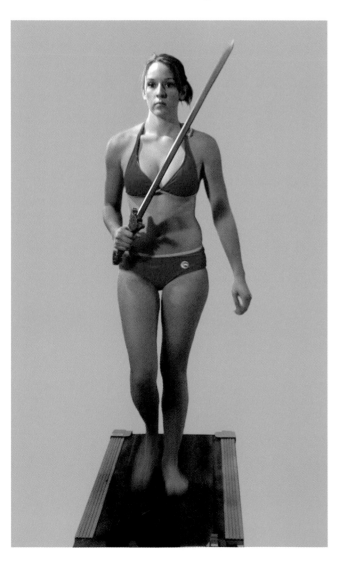

Balancing the Pencil

The best way to achieve delicate, smooth gradations in shading over larger areas on your drawing is to lightly stroke with the side of the graphite rather than pressing the point against the paper. The butter-knife position and the writing position don't work well for light strokes. A better way to hold your pencil is to balance it between your finger and your thumb, as shown in the figure on the right. We will call this the *balanced position*.

In the balanced position, the thumb and the finger act as a hinge. The little finger is then used to gently apply pressure, giving you great control over the amount of graphite that is applied to the drawing with each stroke.

Try using the balanced pencil position to gently shade a large area from light to dark, as shown in the figure on the right.

With a little practice, you should gain very fine control over shading your drawings. Try shading from light to dark and from dark to light with a variety of shapes. As you shade, attempt to keep the shaded areas smooth and clean.

Just the Beginning

I hope this chapter has given you a few things to think about. There is magic in the world if you are willing to look for it. Life can be a beautiful, exciting experience. Sometimes it just needs to be seen. Artists look at the world differently because they train themselves to perceive the world in a more profound way.

In the next few chapters you will be given more insight into artistic perception. You will also have opportunities to practice what you learn with some of the exercises. As you open the world of artistic vision, you will start to see the world in a whole new way.

2

The Benefits of Drawing

Not too long ago, I was asked by some students of mine why I thought drawing was important. I was a little surprised by the question because the students were studying to be computer game artists. The importance of learning to draw was obvious to me, but to them it seemed irrelevant. They didn't realize that even though they would be doing all of their art on a computer, they still needed a foundation in fundamental drawing to really learn how to create great art.

The question did make me think about the issue of learning to draw in a modern computer age. I went back to thinking about why I draw. I also thought about all of the things I have learned from drawing over the years. Let me list just a few of those things here.

- ▶ Drawing has helped me to increase my skill in creating art.
- ▶ Drawing has helped me to understand proportion, value, form, and perspective.
- ▶ Drawing has taught me to plan ahead and patiently follow the plan.
- ▶ Drawing has taught me to focus on the larger elements and then systematically work toward the details.
- ▶ Drawing has given me a way to transfer my vision and my ideas to paper.
- ▶ Drawing has shown me a path to creativity.
- ▶ Drawing has taught me how to control my mind and body for fine, delicate work.
- ▶ Drawing has taught me to relax and enjoy life.
- ▶ Drawing has taught me to look at things as they really are instead of as how I think they should be.
- ▶ Drawing has taught me to understand what I see.

The list could probably go on, but as you can see with just what I have listed, there are plenty of reasons to learn to draw.

Learning from Drawing

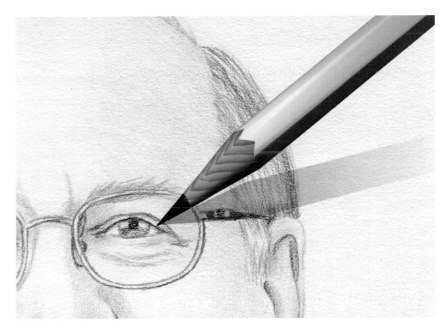

Drawing is at the foundation of art. It is at the heart of almost all the visual arts. Drawing focuses on the very core of the creative process by reducing it to its simplest form. The artist simply uses a pencil and paper to inscribe an image. The quality of the image is completely dependent on the artist's ability to see or imagine and his or her skill in handling a pencil. There is a stark honesty about drawing that is difficult to fake.

Skill in Art

If your goal is to become a better artist, then learning to draw well will be one of the best ways for you to improve. Because drawing is so simple, there is little an artist can do to get around the necessity of understanding the basic elements of art, such as proportion, value, form, and perspective. If you don't know what these terms mean, don't worry; I will go over them in detail later in the book. Just know that they are important artistic terms.

Patience

An artist learns a lot of patience from drawing. Drawing takes time. Sometimes the only way to get the fur coat of a trusted pet to look right in a drawing is to draw each individual strand of hair. Sometimes the only way to accurately draw a busy city street is to painstakingly construct each building in correct perspective to the other buildings. Sometimes the only way to get a portrait to look like the subject is to softly shade the face with delicate gradations. Don't get me wrong; I like quick drawing, but there are times when I am doing a finished drawing where hours might pass while I work on just a part of the drawing.

Planning

Drawing takes planning. I find that I can't draw even simple shapes very well without first working out the shapes lightly on the paper. If the drawing is a complex one, I have to spend a significant amount of time lightly defining each shape. I start with the large, dominant shapes and then work my way to the details.

Communication

Drawing can be a form of communication. Through learning to draw I have increased my ability to communicate. Instead of relying on words alone, I can show people what I mean through the medium of pictures. For example, I often use pictures in this book to explain drawing concepts. I think a book about drawing would be a little remiss if it didn't contain pictures.

A great benefit of drawing is that I can communicate my vision and my ideas to others. Instead of just dreaming about things, I can take a step toward making my dreams real by drawing them. A simple example of this is Jessica, a pirate character that I envisioned. I wanted to create a pirate girl as an example in one of my books about video game art. I first drew her from the front, back, and side.

Later, I used the drawings to build a 3D model of the character.

Creativity

I find that knowing how to draw helps me to be more creative. It isn't so much that drawing makes me more creative; rather, knowing how to draw helps me to be less afraid to create because I have a more direct ability to express my ideas. Have you ever visualized something really cool, but when you tried to draw it or explain it, there seemed to be something lost in the translation? The drawing just didn't match your vision. Do you remember how frustrated you were? Did you give up because you just couldn't bring your ideas to life? How much different would it be if you knew how to draw well?

Control

Drawing requires very tight control over the use of the pencil. In some ways it is like dancing, except that the control is much more delicate, particularly for very fine detail work. Sometimes surgeons will take drawing classes because it helps to train them in small muscle control—that is, the fine movement of the fingers and wrist.

I remember visiting an art museum when there was a traveling show of miniatures. Miniatures are small portraits that were commissioned by nobility before photography was developed. The portrait above is only 13 centimeters wide. The portraits were carried in a locket or other similar device, just like we carry wallet-sized photos of our loved ones today. The show was amazing for the detail of these tiny paintings. I marveled at the skill involved in creating such a tiny painting. Those artists definitely learned control.

Relaxation

Drawing isn't just about control and precise movement. It is also about relaxing and enjoying. Recently, my wife and I took a trip for our anniversary. One of the most enjoyable parts of the trip was spending some time together in a park. We had a book that we were reading together. While she read aloud to me, I sketched the people in the park. I didn't care whether my drawings were good or bad; I didn't even worry about what I drew. I just sketched anything that looked interesting. Not only did I come home feeling rested and rejuvenated, but I also had a record of the vacation in my sketchbook.

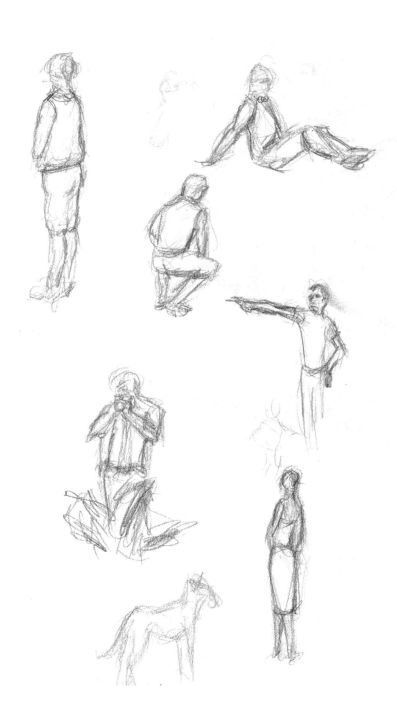

Seeing and Understanding

Probably the most significant thing that I have learned through drawing is to see how things really are instead of how I think they should be. A big revelation for me when I started really learning how to draw was how many assumptions I made in life. Let me give you an example. Take the human eye, which many think is shaped like a football. I have seen many beginning art students draw eyes similar to footballs.

Close examination shows that even though the eye might resemble the shape of a football, it is much more complicated. The eye itself is actually a round sphere within the eye socket. The upper and lower eyelids cover the ball of the eye, allowing only a small portion to be seen. Rarely does the iris of the eye show completely below the upper eyelid. There is a tear duct on the side of the eye near the nose. And the eyelids have thickness, which is most noticeable on the lower lid.

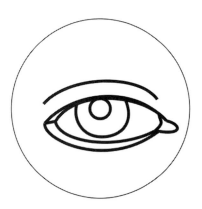

When teaching students how to draw eyes, I first have to unteach the football shape and get them to really look at the eye. As long as they assume they know the shape of the eye, they don't really look at it; they just draw footballs. Once they really start to look at the eye, they begin to understand how it really looks.

I've used the eye as an example, but the principle of seeing things as they really are runs across the board in almost every familiar aspect of our lives. Drawing has taught me to look harder and deeper into everything I draw. No longer do I look at eyes as footballs or fingers as links of sausage. Drawing has forced me to see things as they really are.

With so many benefits from drawing, why doesn't everyone do it? I don't know the answer to why everyone wouldn't want to learn to draw, but I believe that everyone should.

Learning to Draw

Even if you don't think of yourself as an artist, you can still learn to draw. I really believe that. There is no magic that makes one person an artist and another not. Some people might have an aptitude toward drawing and come by it naturally, but that doesn't mean that no one else can learn, any more than thinking that only NASCAR drivers can learn to drive a car. You can do this.

Learning about the Tools

Often people get frustrated with drawing because they are using the wrong tools. A good mechanic will tell you that having the right tools for the job can make all the difference in fixing a problem with your car. The same thing is true with art. If you are using the wrong pencil, paper, or eraser, your drawing will be more difficult. If you use the right pencil, paper, and eraser, your drawing will be easier.

A really good artist can create a good drawing with the charcoal on the burnt end of a stick, but the right tools in the hands of a master can create a masterpiece. Great artists have to understand their tools.

Any form of work and most forms of play require tools of some kind. A writer needs something to write with. A pilot needs an airplane. A hairdresser needs tools to cut and style hair. A mechanic needs tools to work on an engine. A chef needs kitchen utensils. A programmer needs a computer.

The quality of tools you use can make a big difference in your ability to get a job done. I have found that investments in good tools will usually pay for themselves in either time or money.

The Pencil

Almost everyone knows what a pencil is. Pencils are made by the millions and sold in stores ranging from art supply stores to corner convenience stores. When you think of a pencil, you most likely think of a yellow object about seven inches long with an eraser at one end and a sharpened point at the other. Pencils are so basic to our lives that we just assume we understand them. It is interesting to note that the pencil we know today has only been around for a few hundred years.

Selecting a Pencil

The single most important aspect of selecting a pencil is the quality of the graphite. While most pencils do an adequate job for writing a note or doing a quick sketch, they might not be suitable for more refined drawing. When choosing a pencil, you should consider two basic things—the quality and hardness of the graphite.

Graphite Quality

Cheap pencils often have inferior graphite, resulting in many more impurities. These impurities often are found as grit within the graphite, causing the pencil to scratch the drawing surface.

Have you ever noticed while drawing that on occasion the pencil will seem to catch at the paper fibers and not draw as smoothly as before? That is because there is a small piece of grit in the graphite. This grit catches in the paper fibers and causes them to be lifted out of place. If you continue to draw with that pencil, the grit eventually will be released and become embedded in the paper fibers. Then as you continue to draw, the area around the piece of grit forms a small dark area, or hickey, in the drawing. This hickey can be very annoying when you are trying to create the effect of smooth, even shading.

Artist pencils tend to be more refined than common pencils, so the graphite has less grit. While a common pencil might be fine for sketching or doing line drawings, if you are doing any delicate drawing at all, a better-quality pencil should be your choice.

Hard and Soft

The hardness of the graphite affects the amount of graphite that is transferred to the drawing surface. What really happens when you draw is that the graphite from the pencil is rubbed off the pencil and onto the paper. That is why you have to sharpen the pencil from time to time. Harder pencils have more clay mixed with the graphite than softer pencils. This means that less graphite is rubbed off during drawing—the result being a lighter line on the paper.

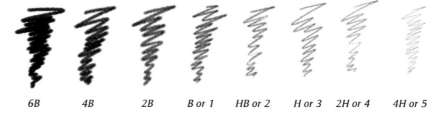

6B   4B   2B   B or 1   HB or 2   H or 3   2H or 4   4H or 5

Pencils have a grading system to show how hard or soft the graphite is. In the United States there are two basic systems: one using numbers alone and the other using numbers and letters. There are, however, no standards among pencil manufacturers, so a 4B pencil from one company may not exactly match a 4B pencil from another.

For most drawing purposes, the softer pencils seem to work better than the harder pencils because they are more flexible in their use. With a soft pencil, the range of dark to light lines and shading can be controlled by the amount of pressure the artist applies when drawing. For example, when the artist needs very light construction lines, very light pressure is applied. When the artist needs darker shading and lines, more pressure is applied.

Harder pencils tend to require more pressure on the paper than softer pencils. When pressure is applied to paper from the pencil, the paper fibers are smashed together. Remember the old detective shows in which the detective wants to read what the last message was on the notepad by the phone? Using a pencil, he lightly shades over the page to reveal what was written before. The reason he can see a message there is because the person who wrote the message smashed the paper fibers when writing the note. The more pressure an artist uses when drawing, the more likely there will be surface damage to the paper.

Smashed paper fibers usually are not a problem when someone is writing, but they can be a real problem when drawing. There is nothing more annoying than a crease appearing in the paper when you are trying to do some smooth shading on a drawing.

Ebony

One of my favorite drawing pencils is called Design Ebony and is made by Sanford. The Design Ebony pencil has a high-quality graphite core with a large diameter. The graphite is very smooth. I have found very little grit in the Design Ebony pencils.

The graphite in the Design Ebony pencil strikes a nice balance between hard and soft. It is soft enough to achieve very dark blacks, while hard enough that it can do light work as well. Many of the drawings in this book were created using the Design Ebony pencil.

Pencil Strokes

Drawings are made up of pencil strokes, which can be bold, light, flowing, or smooth. The stroke you choose for your drawings should be determined by the type of drawing you want to do. Finely rendered drawings use very light, smooth strokes, while cartoons use heavy, bold strokes. The type of pencil strokes an artist uses to create a drawing is a personal choice and is as individual as a person's handwriting. Beginning artists should explore different ways of drawing until they are comfortable with a drawing technique.

A simple zigzag stroke is one of the quickest ways to shade an area. The drawback of a stroke like this is that while it tends to work well for shading flat areas, it does not express much about the nature of the surface. A  zigzag stroke is often used in quick sketches, such as thumbnails or storyboards. Another problem with the zigzag stroke is that the ends of the stroke are darker than the middle.

Another stroke is similar to the zigzag stroke but is created with a more circular scrubbing motion. The stroke is a *buildup stroke*, in which the side of the graphite is lightly rubbed over the paper, building up the darker tones over  time. This stroke is used for fine, smooth gradations in drawings. It is not an expressive stroke; rather, it is a stroke used for smooth shading. When using this method, the artist is attempting to hide any evidence of the individual pencil strokes.

In a *directional stroke*, each stroke is a separate line drawn with the pencil. Directional strokes can be used for shading just like zigzag strokes, but they can be more expressive because they can follow the direction of the shape.  Directional strokes also don't have the disadvantage of being darker at the ends like the zigzag stroke. Directional strokes are used for drawings in which the artist wants to show each stroke of the pencil. They are not used as much when the artist wants smooth, directionless shading.

A variation on the directional stroke is a *weighted directional stroke*. In this stroke, the artist applies more pressure to one end of the stroke than the other. A directional stroke is often used for drawing  ing a lock of hair. Weighted directional strokes are basically a more refined version of the directional stroke and can be used in similar ways.

By changing the direction of the pencil strokes, the artist can create a shading method called *crosshatching*. Crosshatching is a method of using directional strokes that overlap from dif-  ferent directions to create textures or shading. Crosshatching is often used in pen-and-ink drawings.

Sometimes the artist can use pencil strokes to describe an object. These strokes are called *descriptive strokes*. Pencil strokes might be used to create a pine tree, a branch of leaves, or some grass around a rock, among other things. These pencil strokes follow the shape of the object. They are the most descriptive strokes because they not only shade the object, they also show the shape or character of the object.

It is often desirable to keep your drawings consistent and not mix stroke types, but some strokes, such as directional and descriptive, go well together, as in this illustration.

These are just a few types of strokes that an artist can use in drawing. There are as many variations as you can imagine. Try coming up with a few of your own.

Now that you have some idea about pencil strokes, work on a few drawings of things around you. Use your framing card to isolate a couple scenes and try drawing them. Draw the same object a couple of times using different pencil strokes. Notice how the nature of the drawing changes when you use a different technique.

Every problem in life should not always be approached the same. Some problems need different techniques to solve them. The same principle is true in drawing. A detailed portrait might require smooth shading with a minimum of recognizable pencil strokes. On the other hand, a cartoon drawing or a quick thumbnail sketch would not work very well with a smooth shaded approach. If you are struggling with a problem in life or in drawing, try using a different technique.

Paper

Like the pencil, paper is a very important part of drawing. Drawing is actually an abrasive process where the paper acts as the abrasive surface. When a pencil is rubbed against the surface of the paper, some of the graphite from the pencil is rubbed off. With this in mind, it is easy to see why the quality of the paper has a great deal to do with the quality of the drawing.

The more you understand about paper, the better you will be able to select and use the best paper for your drawing projects.

How Paper Is Made

Papermaking is a simple process, yet to make good drawing paper requires a certain amount of skill. Paper is made from fibers—usually cotton or wood fibers, but sometimes other fibers are used. The fibers are separated by a smashing process and suspended in liquid, usually water. The suspended fibers are called *pulp*.

A screen is then passed through the pulp solution. As the screen passes through the pulp, the fibers collect on the screen in a thin sheet. The thickness of the paper is determined by the amount of fibers collected on the screen. When the collected fibers reach the desired thickness, the screen is removed from the pulp solution and the fibers are dried.

The texture of the paper is determined by how the fibers are dried and whether there are any additional smoothing processes. For example, if the fibers are allowed to dry on a drying screen, the finished paper will take on the texture of the screen. This type of paper is often called a *laid finish paper* and is popular as stationery or for documents such as resumes.

Often paper will go through a pressing process to reduce the amount of surface texture. Very smooth papers are pressed using heated presses with high amounts of pressure. Using less heat and less pressure will result in a more uneven surface texture.

Selecting Paper

You should select the paper you use based on the type of drawing you intend to create. If you are creating a highly finished, smooth shaded drawing, the texture of the paper should be very smooth. On the other hand, if you want a textured, rough look to your drawing, you should select a rougher paper. Some papers have a mechanical pattern, while others seem to have a more natural and random texture.

Fibers

Paper is made up of many small, intertwined, threadlike fibers. The most common fiber used in paper is cellulose, made from wood pulp. Wood fibers tend to be short and thus create a more brittle paper. Wood fiber paper also contains acid that causes the paper to deteriorate and turn yellow over time.

Cotton fibers are longer and more flexible than wood fibers. Cotton is also naturally acid-free. Most of the better-quality art papers are made from cotton. Wood fiber paper is getting better but is still considered inferior by most artists.

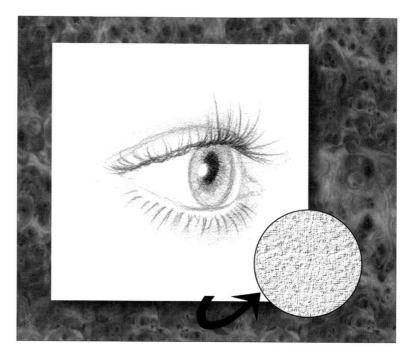

Surface

There are several types of paper surfaces, including hot press, plate, coated, vellum, cold press, rough, and tracing.

Hot Press

Hot-press paper is pressed by hot rollers to create a smooth, hard surface. Hot-press paper is good for fine drawing but might be too smooth for some drawings. Many artists like the smooth texture of hot-press paper because there are seldom irregularities in the paper and it is easier to create smooth shading effects.

Plate

Plate paper is made by a process of pressing paper tightly with a smooth metal plate to create a very smooth, very hard surface. Plate paper is usually not a good choice for drawing paper because it has little texture to grab the graphite. It works better for pen and ink drawings.

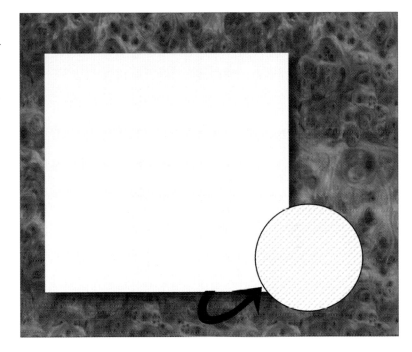

Coated

Coated paper is coated with a thin layer of some nonabsorbent material, such as clay. Coated paper is most often used in printing, where the coating keeps the ink from being absorbed by the paper fibers and spreading. Coated paper usually has a shiny surface that is difficult to draw on.

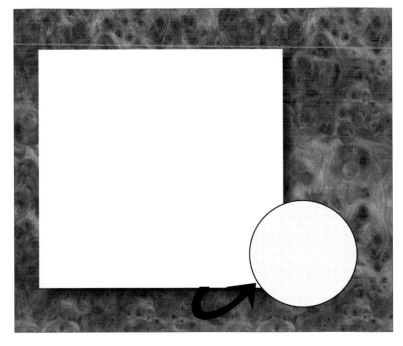

Vellum

A *vellum* surface is good for drawing. The word "vellum" comes from the ancient process of making writing surfaces from the stretched skins of animals. Vellum was the primary writing and drawing surface in Europe prior to the introduction of paper. In describing a surface, the word "vellum" refers to a surface that is similar to the vellum used in ancient times. It has enough texture to hold a pencil line but not so much texture as to interfere with fine shading. The texture is often small so that unwanted patterns don't appear in the drawing.

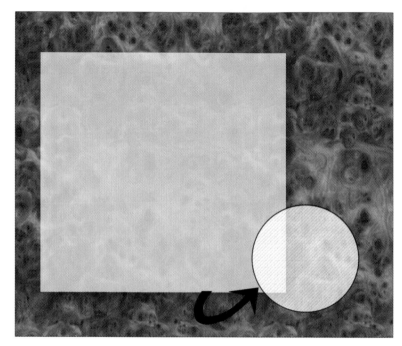

Cold Press

Cold-press paper is pressed with cold rollers. It is generally rougher than vellum or hot-press paper and has a very obvious texture. It is a good drawing paper for sketching and bolder pencil work, but often the texture is too pronounced for fine shading.

Rough

Rough paper is most often used by water-color artists. It has a rough, uneven texture that can create interesting patterns when used for drawings. These patterns become a problem, however, if a smoother shaded finish is desired.

Tracing

Tracing paper is a very smooth, translucent paper used for tracing. It is used by artists when there is a need to transfer all or part of a drawing from one sheet to another, as in animation. Tracing paper has a vellum finish and is sometimes referred to as *tracing vellum*.

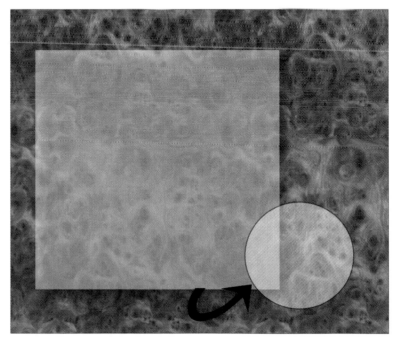

Thickness

The thickness of the paper is also an important consideration when choosing a drawing surface. Thicker paper tends to be stronger than thinner paper because there are more interlocking paper fibers. Thicker paper also has more resistance to pencil pressure, which will reduce the amount of indentations from one page to the next when you are drawing on a pad of paper.

In the United States, paper thickness is measured in weight per ream. A ream is 500 sheets of paper. For example, if 500 sheets of paper weighed 200 pounds, then the paper would be labeled 200-lb paper. The drawback to this kind of measuring system is that not all paper is the same size, so a 200-lb paper from one company might not be the same as a 200-lb paper from another company.

Acid

Acid content in paper will cause the paper to turn yellow and become brittle over time. Most of the better drawing paper is acid-free, which means that there is either no acid in the fibers or that buffers have been added to the paper to offset the acid content. Paper made from cotton is naturally acid-free. Make sure you choose an acid-free paper when you are doing a finished drawing. Some drawing paper, such as newsprint paper (inexpensive paper used for sketching), is not acid-free. Newsprint paper is not generally used for finished drawings.

Tooth

"Tooth" is a word many artists use to describe the abrasive qualities of a paper. A paper's tooth refers to how much graphite the paper will scrub off from the pencil. Some papers have little tooth, causing the graphite to appear light on the paper, while other papers have a great deal of tooth, causing the graphite to come off the pencil faster.

More than anything, tooth is a matter of comfort for the artist. Some artists like a lot of tooth in their paper and some like little. If you like to create delicate drawings, selecting a paper with little tooth might be your best choice. If you like to be bold and direct in your drawings, greater tooth might be a better choice.

Color

Some drawing paper is colored. Colored paper is not generally used for pencil drawings. It is more commonly used for charcoal or pastel drawings, where there are both darker and lighter media than the color of the paper. Using colored paper for a pencil drawing limits the amount of light-to-dark contrast in the picture because the lightest part of the drawing is the paper.

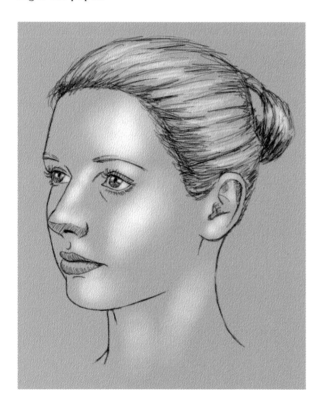

Testing Papers

If you can test a few papers before you choose one to draw on, you will have a much better idea of how the paper will react to the pencil. Sometimes art supply stores will have small sample squares of paper that you can test right in the store. To test the paper, take a soft pencil (2B or softer) and lightly scrub the side of the graphite across the paper. The softer the graphite in the pencil is, the easier it will be to see the pattern and texture of the paper. Notice the pattern of the paper's texture and how well the paper takes the graphite. A good drawing paper will receive the graphite in a smooth, even manner and it will be easy to blend your strokes. Poor drawing papers will make it more difficult to blend strokes.

Be Good to Your Paper

Be good to your paper, and your paper will be good to you. Paper fibers are delicate and become damaged very easily. Harsh drawing and excessive erasing destroy the surface quality of the paper. Once the paper is damaged, it can't be repaired.

Damaged paper creates an uneven drawing surface. The damaged area will receive the graphite differently than the undamaged areas. If the paper fibers are raised by the abrasive use of an eraser, the damaged area will have more tooth than the surrounding paper. It is almost impossible to compensate for damaged areas when doing delicate pencil work.

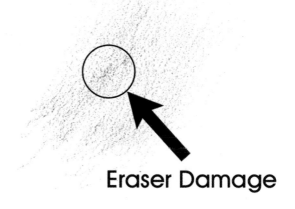

Eraser Damage

A common mistake of beginning artists is to use the eraser too frequently. Experienced artists tend to rarely erase. If you must erase an area, the best eraser to use is a kneaded eraser. Kneaded erasers are less abrasive than other erasers and they leave less residue behind. They also can be molded to any shape—a useful trait when you want to do fine touchup work on your drawing.

Your hand can also cause problems with the drawing surface. The pores in the skin of the hand secrete oil. The oil is used by the body to keep our skin soft. Without the oil, the skin of our hands would be rough and tend to crack. Though this oil is good for our hands, it is not good for drawing paper. The oil from your hand can cause slick spots on the paper that won't receive graphite as well as the rest of the paper. The best way to avoid oil from your hand get-

ting on your paper is to use a barrier piece of paper between your hand and the drawing surface.

The barrier paper serves two purposes. The first is that it keeps oil from your hand from getting on the paper. The second is that it helps to prevent smearing. I often see work from beginning and sometimes even advanced artists with smears and smudges on it.

Erasers

I mention erasers last because while they might be necessary, they should be used sparingly. Erasing can cause paper damage, so the less you erase your picture, the better.

Erasers come in many different shapes and types, most of which are not good for use on delicate drawing paper. The less abrasive the eraser, the better it will be to use on your drawings. *Never* use the eraser that comes on the end of a pencil. Most of the time these erasers are cheap and tend to not only be highly abrasive, but they also will, on occasion, smear the picture rather than clean it. This is especially true of some of the cheaper pencils.

The eraser most commonly used by artists is a kneaded eraser. The name "kneaded" comes from the fact that the eraser is malleable, like bread dough. Being malleable, the eraser can be molded into almost any shape imaginable, from a sharp point for detailed touchups to a broad wedge for large cleanups.

Kneaded erasers are usually much less abrasive than other erasers. The better ones will have a fine, even texture. Some of the cheaper ones will feel gritty.

All erasers leave a residue on the paper. A kneaded eraser leaves very fine particles, almost like sand. Other types of erasers will often leave large particles on the paper. To remove the residue, you need to brush the drawing very lightly with a finger or a soft brush. Sometimes blowing on the paper will remove most of the residue, but usually not all of it. You should be very careful when removing residue so that you don't smear any of your drawing.

Drawing

Now that you know a little about the tools you need for drawing, it is time to do some testing to see what you like. Try out some different papers with a few different pencils. Get a feel for how they work together.

You should start keeping a sketchbook. Buy something that you can take with you. Set a goal to draw something in your sketchbook every day. For now, don't worry too much about the quality of your drawings. You are still getting used to the tools and techniques. As you progress in this book, you will begin to see some improvement by following the exercises.

3

Seeing Light

L ight is essential to sight. Without light there is no sight, at least not with our natural eyes. Because drawing begins with seeing, a book about drawing should have some significant information on the nature of light and how our eyes perceive it. Understanding how light works on objects in a scene helps the artist create a feeling of depth and substance in a drawing. Artists can also use light to add drama and feeling to a drawing.

But light goes far beyond just seeing. Light is also essential for our existence. Other than a few fungi, plants need light to grow. Without light our food supply would end because plant life is at the foundation of our ecosystem. Almost every power source used today utilizes light in some way. For example, many of our power plants use heat for powering the generators to generate electricity. Heat is basically infrared light. Light from the sun plays a big role in our weather patterns because it heats our atmosphere. Light is a core element of our existence.

We also need light emotionally. Annually in the United States, there are more cases of depression in the winter months than in the summer months. This condition, known as *Seasonal Affective Disorder* or *SAD*, afflicts many individuals every year.

Types of Light

There are basically two types of light in drawing—direct light and reflected light. Direct light emanates from a light source, such as a light bulb or the sun. During a normal sunny day, the world is bathed in light with the sun as the light source. If you were to look directly at the sun (something your mother probably told you not to do), you would be looking at direct light. The same thing is true for a lightbulb or a campfire. Anything that creates light, such as a TV or a computer monitor, is giving off direct light.

Reflected light bounces off of objects. We see the world around us primarily through reflected light. The yellow, green, and red in the picture below are all reflected light. The light of the sun is bouncing from the trees and reflecting back to the viewer.

 **Direct Light**

Light Source

©istockphoto.com/Vera Bogaerts

Absorption, Reflection, and Pass Through

Light travels in a straight path from the light source until it hits something. When light hits an object it will do one of three things: It will bounce off the object, it will be absorbed by the object, or it will pass through the object. In the picture light is coming from the sun. When light hits the blue object, blue light is reflected to the viewer's eyes. All non-blue light is absorbed into the object.

The color of an object is determined by the light that is absorbed into it and the light that is reflected off of it. A white light contains all colors of visible light. If a white light strikes a blue object, all colors other than those that are blue will be drawn into the object and will form heat. The blue light is reflected.

Have you ever noticed that black clothing is much hotter to wear on a sunny day than white clothing? That is because black absorbs all of the visible light and doesn't reflect any light. When light is absorbed into a surface, it creates heat. On the other hand, a white shirt reflects all of the light of the visible spectrum.

If the object is transparent, some of the light will pass through the object. In the case of a transparent object, such as glass, almost all of the light will pass through the object. The picture shows light passing through the blue object.

Not only is blue light reflected, but it is also the only light that passes through the blue object. All of the light is absorbed into the blue object.

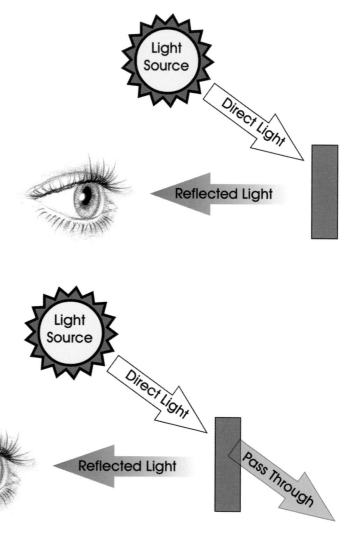

Light and Shadow

When there is light there is also shadow. A *shadow* is an area of diminished light because the object is blocking some of the light from entering. The light and shadow of an object help show its shape and dimensions. In this picture, the shadow gives the figure the appearance of standing on the ground, even though the figure is only seen in silhouette.

Now let's take a look at how light defines a three-dimensional object. We will start with a simple shape, such as a sphere. Try drawing this picture of a ball sitting on a tabletop before you go on to the rest of the chapter.

Highlight

The *highlight* of an object is the part that light directly reflects from the light source to the viewer's eyes. The highlight is located on the brightest area of the ball, as shown in this picture. The highlight area is at a direct reflection angle from the light source. If you are using white paper and a pencil, the highlight will generally be left as the white of the paper. For this reason, you don't actually draw the highlight; rather, you draw the rest of the object and leave the highlight.

Highlight

Raking Light

The area that surrounds the highlight where the light is not as directly reflected is called *raking light*. The name comes from the way the light skims across the surface and hits it at an angle. This area extends outward from the highlight and gradually gets darker because the surface of the object is curving away from the light.

Raking light

Light Area

The area that contains the highlight and the raking light is the *light area* of an object. Most objects can be defined as having a light area and a shadow area. Because the light area receives the most light, most of the detail in a drawing is in this area.

Light area

Shadow Area

As the surface of the ball turns away from the light source, it no longer receives light directly from the light source. All of the area that does not receive direct light from the light source is called the *shadow area*. The shadow area generally receives the least amount of detail in a drawing because there is less light to define this area.

Shadow area

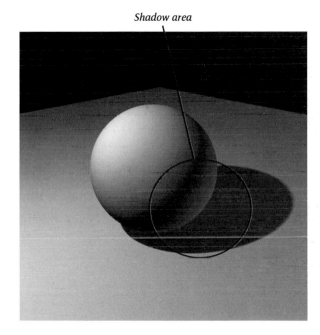

In situations where there is only one light shining on an object, such as a ball, roughly half of the ball will be in the shadow area and half will be in the light area. Viewing the ball directly to the side of the light source illustrates how the light and shadow areas are divided.

Light side   Dark side

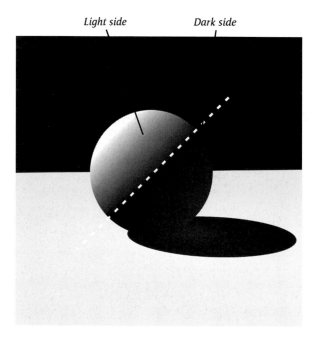

Core Shadow

There is a band of shadow that separates the raking light from the shadow area of the ball. This shadow is called the *core shadow*. The core shadow runs along the edge of the object that is directly past the influence of the light. It is a very important shadow for the artist because the core shadow, more than any other shading, defines the form. The core shadow is the darkest shadow on the ball because it receives the least amount of light.

Core shadow

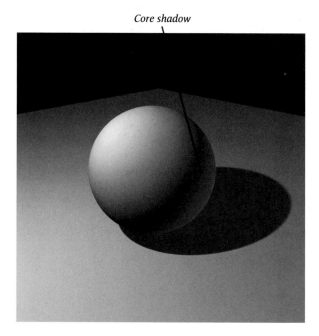

Reflected Light

The shadow area does not receive direct light from the light source, but it does receive indirect light. Indirect light is reflected from other surfaces onto the ball. In the picture of the ball, the light that hits the table and reflects back to us also reflects back toward the ball. The reflected light gives definition to the shadow area of a drawing.

Reflected light

Cast Shadow

Because the ball interrupts some of the light traveling from the light source to the table, there is an area of shadow on the table. This area of shadow is called the *cast shadow*.

Cast shadow

Cast shadows are not just flat shadows. They have unique characteristics that an artist must understand to make them look correct. As the shadow becomes more distant from the object, the edge becomes less distinct. This happens because there is more chance for reflected light to reach the shadow area. The shadow has a diffused edge.

There is also a slightly lighter area just beneath the ball. This area is the twice-reflected light area. The light that is reflected to the ball bounces off the ball and into the cast shadow area, giving that area a small amount of light. This is one reason why some cast shadows seem to be lighter near the middle.

Diffused edge

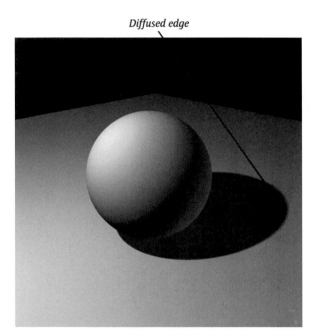

Twice-reflected light

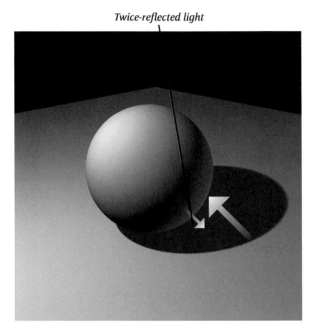

Front and Rim Lighting

Many artists like to light their scenes with the light coming from behind the artist and to the side so they can show most of the light but also some of the shadow areas. This type of lighting best defines the form of the objects in their drawings. Lighting from the front or the back of the object tends to flatten the form of the object, as shown here. However, sometimes these types of lighting effects can add drama to a drawing, especially in the case of rim lighting.

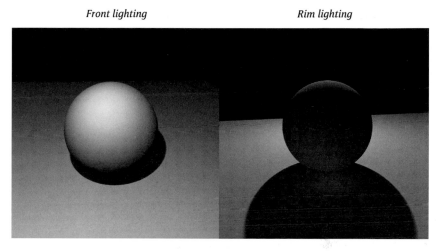

Front lighting *Rim lighting*

Multiple Light Sources

Many times, objects we see in life have more than one light source. This is particularly true of characters or objects that are in interior settings. A single

room inside a building might have many lights illuminating a character or object from multiple angles. Each light will have an effect on how the character or object looks. This can often be confusing for the artist who has to track the direction of the lights to understand the angles of the lights. The picture on the left shows the ball with three lights. Notice the multiple cast shadows. The cast shadows are the best clue for determining the number and location of all the lights hitting the object.

Did you realize there was so much involved in the lighting of a simple ball? We see light every day, but unless we are familiar with its nature, we might miss many aspects. Try drawing the ball again, and this time use what you have just learned about light to define the lighting of the ball. Compare your drawings. Was your second drawing a better depiction of the ball?

We are not done yet. There is still a lot more to learn about light.

Shapes

So far we have talked about lighting a ball. Now let's see how light affects other shapes. This picture shows three other shapes using the same lighting that was used for the ball. Can you find the different aspects of light and shadow on each? What are the light areas and what are the shadow areas? Where is the highlight? What about the core shadow?

Try drawing each shape and see how you do. Notice that the cube has flat panels of shading that go evenly from a lighter area to a darker area. The core shadow on the cone runs from the cone's point to its base in a straight line. The more complex dough-nut shape has a core shadow that twists with the shape of the object. Each shape has its own way of capturing light.

No matter what the shape is, the principles of light and shadow still apply. Look at the picture of the cheerleader on the next page. The nose is a feature that beginning artists struggle with. If you look at a nose closely, you will notice that it is basically a cone with a ball on the end and another ball on either side. Can you find the core shadow and the reflected light on her nose? Notice that there is also reflected light on her chin.

Okay, now it is time to get up and look around you a little bit. See if you can see the elements of light and shadow. Do you see any highlights? What about reflected light? Can you spot the core shadows? Finding the cast shadows should be easy, but can you find the twice-reflected light within the shadow and the diffused edges of the shadow?

If you are having trouble, eliminate all light sources except one. Don't get confused because of multiple light sources.

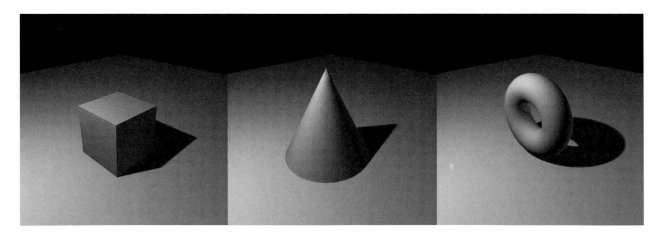

Surface Qualities

In real life, every surface has a texture. Sometimes the texture is only a color, whereas other times it might be very complex, such as the bark of a tree. Take a quick look around and study some of the many textures you see in everyday life. You will notice on close examination that every surface has some qualities that you can fit into a few specific categories.

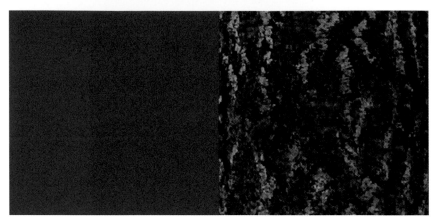

©Richard Polak, http://www.environment-textures.com

- ► **Color**
- ► **Roughness**
- ► **Translucency**
- ► **Reflectivity**
- ► **Luminance**

Each one of these qualities or attributes is part of what gives the surface the look and feel it has. To make a drawing look believable, the artist needs to capture the inherent qualities of the surfaces he or she is trying to depict by drawing textures that match the surface as closely as possible. The metallic sheen of a kitchen appliance has a very different look than a weathered fencepost does. The hard grey of a sidewalk is very different than the spiky look of the lawn right next to it. Look at this picture and see whether you can tell what the objects are based on just the texture.

©Richard Polak, http://www.environment-textures.com

Color

One of the most noticeable characteristics of any surface is its color. We often refer to an object by its color. We say "the red car" or "the blue sweater." Some colors are tied to emotional states. We call a person who is on a lucky streak "red hot" or a person who is depressed "blue." We even assign temperatures to colors. Red, yellow, and orange are considered warm colors, while purple, blue, and green are thought of as cool colors. Although this is a book about drawing so most of your work will be in black and white, there are still a few things that you should understand about color. For example, how does color affect the value (light and dark) of an object? A red ball, for instance, will have a very different value than a white ball or even a black ball.

The three top pictures show the red ball next to a white ball and a black ball. In the bottom three, the red ball is now in black and white. Notice how much darker the red ball is than the white ball. Also notice that the red ball is still quite a bit brighter than the black ball. Colors such as red and blue are naturally darker than colors such as yellow.

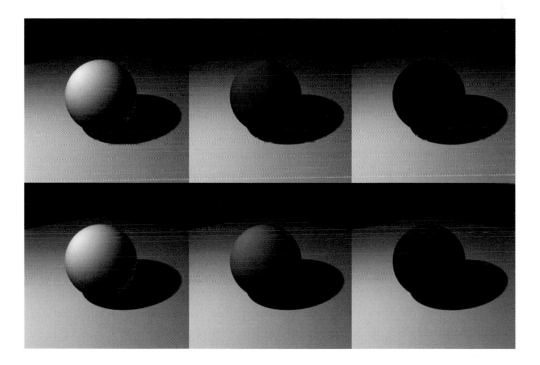

How Light Affects Colors

The light that your eyes process so you can see the world around you is called the *visible band* of light. The visible band of light is made up of a spectrum of colors. If you have ever seen a rainbow, you have seen the spectrum of visible light. Rainbows are made from light bouncing off water particles in the air. Because each color has its own unique characteristics, some colors are bounced in one direction and some are bounced in another, forming bands of pure color. These bands of color are always in the same order, with red at one end and violet or purple at the other end. All the rest of the colors are between those two colors.

©istockphoto.com/Michelle Radin

Roughness in Textures

Every surface you see in real life has some degree of roughness. Some surfaces, such as glass or polished metal, have such a low degree of roughness that it can only be seen using a microscope. Other surfaces, such as a rock wall or gravel, have noticeable roughness. The rougher a surface is, the more it refracts light. *Refraction* is the scattering of light when it hits an uneven surface. When light hits a surface, it bounces off the surface at a direct angle from the light source.

Translucency in Textures

In nature, not all surfaces are opaque; some surfaces are translucent. A translucent surface allows some amount of light to pass through it, making it possible to see through the surface. This picture shows a good example of a translucent surface. Notice how the glass of the pyramid changes the color and detail of the building seen through it.

So what would happen to the lighting of the ball if it were translucent? Look at the picture on the right. Notice how some of the light passes through the ball. This makes it so you can see both the front and back of the ball through the ball. It also makes it so you see the table on the other side of the ball, including the shadow of the ball. The highlight, core shadow, reflected light, and other aspects of light and shadow don't go away just because the object is translucent.

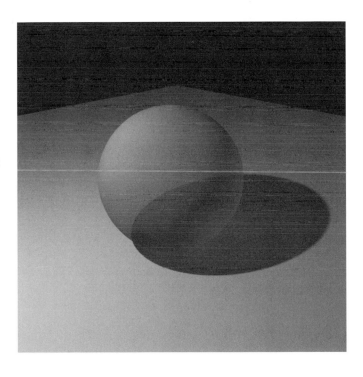

Reflectivity in Textures

Reflectivity is related to roughness in textures. The more even and polished a surface is, the more it will tend to reflect light directly back to the viewer. A reflective surface acts like a mirror, reflecting its surroundings back to our eyes. Reflections are more complicated to draw than any other aspect of a surface because they are like drawing a picture within a picture.

If the ball is reflective, it will still have the same light and shadow properties, but it will be more defined and the surface will reflect an image of the surrounding area back to you. Notice the strong highlight. The highlight is reflecting the light source directly to us. The line across the middle of the ball is a reflection of the near end of the table.

Now let's take a look at what happens when the table is reflective also. You can see the reflection of the ball just below the ball on the table. Reflections on flat surfaces are like mirrors and reflect directly the objects around them.

If you change the object to something more complex, the reflection becomes even more complex. The doughnut shape here is shiny and so is the table. The table is being reflected in the doughnut, and the doughnut is being reflected in the table.

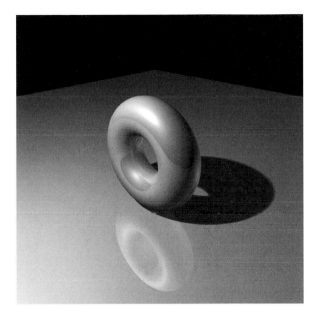

To better see how reflection works, let's place the ball on a wooden texture. Basically, you are starting to combine some of the concepts of surface qualities. Notice that the reflection of the wood grain from the table is on the underside of the ball. The reflected light also changes to a warmer brown because only the brown of the table is reflected from the table.

Okay, now let's change the white ball for a stone one. Notice that all of the principles of light, shadow, and reflection are still there, but they are within the context of the surface of the stone ball.

Try drawing the stone ball and see whether you can get the texture to look right with the lighting. Unless you see only in black and white, you will have to translate the world of color around you into black and white when you draw. This picture is of the stone ball now in black and white. Does your drawing look similar to the black-and-white picture?

Okay, now I'll really give you a challenge. How about drawing a transparent stone ball on a wooden table? Won't that be fun?! Well, here you go. Give this picture a try and see how you do.

Surface Luminance

Surface luminance is the brightness of an object. For example, a light bulb will have a high degree of luminance when the light is turned on and no luminance when it is turned off. Luminance is a direct light source. If something is bright, such as a computer monitor, there will be no light and shadow properties unless there is a brighter light shining on the monitor. Take a look at what happens when the ball on the wooden table is changed to a globe of light. Notice that there are no cast shadows from the ball. It might be said to have a highlight, but there is no core shadow or any other kind of shadow because there is no shadow area.

Putting It Together

We have covered a lot of ground here. I hope you've gained a better understanding of how light works and how we see things because of it. Now it is time to practice what we have talked about in this chapter. Try drawing the soccer ball. As you draw, remember that the highlight will be the white of your paper. Everything else will be darker.

4

Developing Vision through Drawing

So far in this book we have covered a lot of concepts about seeing. From here on out, we will be looking at drawing. Drawing is related to seeing in that it is an expression of sight. Sometimes the drawing comes from sight and sometimes it comes from insight. I have found that is usually a combination of both.

Drawing is also a skill, and like many other skills, it takes practice. To draw well you have to practice drawing. With practice, many aspects of drawing can be mastered even by those who initially have very little skill in the art. If you have drawn as suggested in the book thus far, you probably have already seen some improvement in your work. This chapter should help greatly with your progress.

Two Steps

Drawing can be broken down into two major steps: blocking and shading. *Blocking* is the process of defining the elements in the drawing with light construction lines. It is often called *blocking in a drawing*. *Shading* is the process of defining the values in a drawing. It encompasses lighting and color.

Blocking in a drawing is the first step in defining what the drawing will become. During this stage the artist uses lightly drawn lines to define the elements of the drawing. The composition is determined, the major shapes are defined, and the proportions of each element in the picture are delineated. It is basically like creating a plan for the drawing.

In life we create plans for a lot of things. An architect draws house plans. Entrepreneurs create business plans. We plan our vacations, our retirement, and weddings. We even plan our meals. The reason we plan these things is so that we can project the outcome of our efforts with some degree of accuracy. So doesn't it make sense for us to plan a drawing if we want the drawing to be good?

With few exceptions, drawings can be broken down into basic shapes. Defining elements of a drawing into basic shapes helps the artist understand the nature of each form. By understanding the nature of each form, the artist is better equipped to set up the drawing.

Although most drawings are representations of three-dimensional scenes, the drawing itself is a two-dimensional picture of shaded shapes. These shapes often overlap in a drawing, which helps give the drawing a three-dimensional look.

Measuring Your Drawing

If you are using a photographic reference, you can measure and compare directly your drawing and the photograph because both are flat images and all you need to do is to scale the drawing up or down from the photograph. In life it is a little more complicated because you can't lay a ruler down on a scene. When drawing in life, artists often use a method of measuring using their pencil and thumb as a guide. Let me explain how it works.

1 First, hold your pencil up at arm's length in the butter-knife position, looking at the scene you intend to draw. Use the pencil to measure distances in the scene as if it were a ruler measuring a photograph. Use the top of the pencil to line it up with the top of what you want to measure. Now, place your thumb along the pencil at the place that marks the bottom of the element you are measuring. The image below shows you how to hold your pencil when measuring a scene.

Most of us will not have our arms change radically in length while doing one drawing. By always holding your pencil at arm's length and sighting between the top of the pencil and where your thumb is, you will be able to compare the measured object with other objects in the scene.

2 The lines should still be light. If you draw too heavy at the beginning of your drawing, you will find yourself trapped into having some dark lines that you really don't want. It is better to define the drawing as lightly as possible and then add the heavier lines during the shading process.

Unwanted line

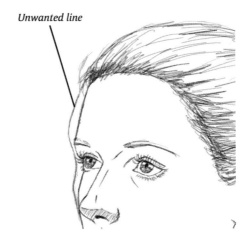

Blocking in a Drawing

The first step to creating a drawing is to block in the major shapes. Blocking in a drawing is lightly indicating with the pencil how the drawing will fit within the picture plane. All of the major elements of the drawing are laid out in an outline form. The artist starts out loosely defining the major features of the drawing, and then refines them until they become an accurate guide for the finished rendering. Let's get started.

©istockphoto.co/Jeremy Voisey

1 Use the picture of the castle turret as reference for a drawing. Start by quickly defining the shapes.

Note

Don't draw as heavily as the picture above. I had to purposely darken the lines because they were so light that they wouldn't print. Usually when drawing, the initial lines are very light.

If you think the drawing looks like a bunch of scribbles, you are right. At this early stage the main concern is to get the drawing started, not to accurately draw each line. The goal of the first few lines is to fit everything in the picture plane. A common mistake that beginning artists make is to start drawing at one end of the paper and work their way across. I can't tell you how many times in a beginning drawing class I see pictures of people cut off at the knees or drawings that don't fit the paper adequately. All of this can be avoided by simply defining the drawing with a few light lines defining the major shapes.

2 Notice that the ovals for the turret are drawn through the building. When drawing an oval, stopping at the edge of the wall can interrupt the flow of the oval. Drawing through an object in your drawings is a good way to construct your pictures because it helps to better define the objects.

3 The next step in blocking in a drawing is to use the initial lines as a guide for defining the actual elements in it. You still don't have to be absolutely accurate, but you need to start moving in that direction. This is where you need to start measuring and comparing so you can define the general proportions of the turret compared to the other elements in the picture. How wide is the turret compared to its height? How far apart are the windows? Measure the elements in the reference photo and then measure your drawing and see whether the proportions match.

During the blocking-in stage of your drawing, it is important that you work toward creating a clear and detailed plan for your drawing. As with almost anything in life, planning is important. On average you should spend about half of your drawing time blocking in your drawing. Some complex pictures might take more planning time than simple pictures. If you are new to drawing, more time should be spent in the planning phase to ensure that the finished drawing matches your vision. Be patient. Time spent working out the problems up front will pay big dividends later in your drawing.

For those readers who like to rush into things, blocking in your drawing might be difficult. Just remember that you are learning a discipline that will serve you well in many facets of your life. Try to slow down and enjoy the process. Learn to enjoy the present challenge before you rush on to the next.

For those readers who love to plan but never act, we will deal with you later, when we get to the shading stage.

Though the planning of the drawing might only account for around 50 percent of your drawing time, my guess is that this stage will account for around 75 percent of the quality of your drawing. Of course these figures are debatable, but you can use them as a guide when drawing.

Just like in life, inadequate planning often results in substandard quality. If you want to improve quality in anything, first look at the planning and see whether it is adequate for the project. Too often beginning artists want to jump right in and start shading and rendering when they haven't given enough thought to planning their drawings. This almost always results in frustration on the part of the artist because the drawing is out of proportion or the composition is lacking.

4 Once you have the picture generally defined, it is time to create a more accurate drawing over the top of what you already have. If you followed my advice and drew the initial lines very lightly, you should not have to worry about erasing them when you draw over them at this stage. Make the more accurate drawing just a little

darker so it stands out more, but don't overdo it. The lines still need to be light. Remember, you are creating a plan for your drawing, rather than the finished shading.

This is when I will generally pull out a straight edge to define straight lines in my drawings. Using a straight edge, such as a ruler, is the best way to draw straight lines. You are not cheating if you use a straight edge when you draw, so don't get hung up on that.

Every drawing has to be accurate but some require more accuracy than others. It's a good habit to do a lot of measuring and comparing when drawing, especially for beginning artists. As you become more comfortable with drawing, you will measure your drawings without a lot of conscious thought because it will become natural for you to compare things. You might not even notice you are doing it.

Shading

This is the moment some of you have been waiting for. It is time to start shading the drawing. Your drawing should now be a detailed plan of the finished drawing. The lines should be light enough that they will not interfere with shading, but dark enough that you can see them clearly.

Shading the drawing is the process of drawing light and color as values from the darkest area of your drawing to the white of your paper. A good way to start shading your drawing is to look for the part of your drawing that you want to be the darkest area on it. In this case I chose the dark areas around the windows and lower lip of the roof. By defining the darkest area first, you can establish that all other shading will be values between that area and the white of the paper. This will help you gauge how dark to draw the other areas of the drawing.

For those readers who lack confidence in themselves, this stage might be the scariest because you will be committing yourself to the drawing. No more will you be using light, almost imperceptible lines. In the shading stage you will boldly apply graphite to the paper.

Like everything in life, there comes a time when the planning is finished and it is time to act. But unlike some things in life, this is not a matter of life and death. It is just a drawing. Try to stay loose and just work at shading step by step.

Shading is fairly delicate work, and it is important that you not smudge the drawing where you rest your hand on the paper. Remember to place a blank piece of paper between your hand and the drawing to help reduce smudging.

Even though the turret has many windows and other decorative elements, it is basically a cylinder. As you shade, look for the core shadow and the reflected light along the right side of the turret. You can see it lightly in the photograph, but emphasizing it in your drawing will give the drawing a more three-dimensional look.

1 Start laying in some of the shading in the surrounding area of the turret and the two other turrets in the background. Remember to look for the shadow elements you learned in Chapter 3. Can you see that the entire right wall is lit with reflected light? Can you see the cast shadows on the windows and some of the stonework on the left side of the turret?

2 Continue to shade the drawing until you have everything shaded similar to the picture. For now you don't need to worry about the ivy growing on the building; that will come later. Right now all you need to worry about are the light areas and the shadow areas. The idea is to define and shade these areas first and then add the detail.

3 When creating a drawing, it is important to establish the lighting before you continue with the detail. Establishing the lighting of the scene will help to keep the values consistent. Often I see drawings in which the reflected light is too bright or the details in the light areas are too dark. A good drawing has consistent lighting. The shadow areas are in shadow, and the light areas are in light. The core shadow runs along the edge of the shadow area next to the light area. The highlights are consistent with the light source. Learn to establish the lighting as the first step in shading your drawings.

4 Now you can go in and draw the ivy and add some detail to the rest of the drawing. Notice that the ivy is darker than the surrounding stone of the building. In the color photograph it might be a little confusing, but where the stone is primarily a yellowish-brown the ivy is a reddish-orange, a darker color.

5 You don't need to draw every brick in the building and every shingle on the roof to indicate that the building is made from brick and the roof has shingles. A few lines indicating the bricks and a few texture lines on the roof will give the appearance of stonework and shingles.

Organic Drawings

While the turret had some curves and a variety of shapes, it was a man-made object. In drawing and art, subjects are sometimes referred to as being *organic* or *inorganic*. Inorganic subjects in drawings are those that tend to be more geometric in nature, such as buildings, machinery, and other manmade elements. Organic subjects in drawings are those that have few or no geometric elements.

The next example for you to follow is an organic subject. This picture is of some friendly ducks in the city park. While there are some organic shapes, such as the ovals of the body and head, the duck is made up of mostly organic curves.

1 Starting the drawing is very similar to how you started the turret in the last example. Begin by loosely defining the size and shape of the duck on the paper using very light construction lines. Define the oval of the body and the curve of the neck leading up to the head. Draw in the wedge of the bill and the feet. Indicate the tail feathers and folded wings.

This drawing does not have as many individual shapes as the turret and should be easier to lay out in a few quick lines on the paper. Focus mostly on proportions. Make sure that the head is in the right place with regard to the rest of the duck and that it is the right size.

2 Over the top of the initial lines, draw in a more accurate drawing of the shape of the duck. Define the outer edges of the duck and try to get them to match the photograph as closely as possible. Notice that some edges overlap each other, such as the back of the neck overlapping the body and the body overlapping the legs.

3 Start adding some features to the head and other parts of the drawing, such as the wings, tail feathers, and feet.

At this point you should still be defining shapes and doing a lot of measuring so your plan for the duck will be as accurate as possible. Compare the head to the feet and the body. Make sure the duck's proportions are as correct as you can make them.

4 The duck has many distinct markings. When the proportions of the duck feel correct, move on and establish some guidelines for the individual feathers and some of the markings around the eyes and head. You don't have to draw in every feather exactly where it is in the photograph, but the feathers need to be similar in their number and locations.

Remember that you are drawing a plan for the finished picture of a duck. Try to be as accurate as you can.

5 Like in the drawing of the turret, when the plan for the drawing is ready, it is time to establish the lighting of the drawing. In this case I didn't start with the darkest darks; rather, I lightly shaded in the basic lighting of the duck. This gave me a basic idea of the shape and form of the body, neck, and head.

Even though it is not as pronounced as it will be in the end, establishing the lighting helps give you an understanding of the form as you create the many patterns and markings of the duck's feathers. If you pushed the darks all the way, you would lose much of the detail you established in the blocking-in phase.

6 The duck is standing in the shade of a tree. There are some areas of the duck that are lit with direct sunlight streaming through breaks in the leaves. These are most noticeable around the back of the neck and the tail feathers. Emphasizing these lighted areas will only cause the viewer confusion. Instead, try to treat these areas with restraint, so they are not as obvious as they are in the photograph.

7 Once the lighting is established, start working on the details and patterns on the duck. Develop the areas of the head and bill. Start with the eye and move outward from there.

Whenever I create a drawing of a person or an animal, I always tend to start the detail with the eyes. We tend to look at eyes. Maybe this is because it is natural for us to look to see whether a person or an animal is looking at us. It is a form of communication. If a person is looking elsewhere or not paying attention, our first clue generally comes from the person's eyes.

8 The next big step is to shade in all the patterns and markings in the neck and body of the duck. This is where the detail from blocking in the feathers in the beginning stages will be a great help. Start with the patterns of the small feathers around the neck, and then work your way across the body. Notice that the small feathers tend to create patterns, whereas the larger feathers have individual markings.

The edges of many of the duck's feathers, especially on the wings, are lighter than the rest of the feather. Drawing these lighter areas requires you to draw around them. Drawing around lighter areas is preferable to coming in later and erasing.

You might be tempted to shade in the entire area and then come back and use an eraser to define the lighter areas later. I tend to avoid using an eraser for anything except cleaning up a drawing when I am finished. Erasers tend to smudge the drawing and reverse the pattern of the paper.

The pattern on drawing paper is like a series of hills and valleys. When you draw, the graphite catches on the hills, leaving the valleys relatively clean. The more graphite you add, the more the valleys are filled in. When you later come back with an eraser, the graphite on the hills is removed and the valleys retain the graphite. This reverses the pattern on the paper. I know this sounds a little picky, but it can have a very subtle effect on a drawing.

9 In this last step to drawing the duck, add the dark of the cast shadow below the body, around the feet. The cast shadow is indistinct in my drawing because I am using it to define the feet and lift the duck so it looks more three-dimensional. Because of the lighting in the photograph, there is no distinct cast shadow below the duck.

By fading the shadow as it goes farther from the center of the picture, I create a vignette—a picture that blends into the background rather than continuing on to the edge of the picture. You might have noticed that both pictures in this chapter are vignettes. This is because it is an easy way to compose a drawing. Chapter 6, "Composition," will discuss composition to help you design the entire picture plane.

Hopefully you now have two nice drawings—one of a turret and one of a duck. Yours might even be better than the examples in this book. I hope you did well. If you struggled, you can always try again. The more you practice with a single subject, the better you will become at drawing that subject.

Try drawing this sculpture of a head and see how you do. Art universities often have art students draw from sculptures rather than from people because all of the surface detail is the same color. This focuses the student's attention on lighting rather than allowing them to be distracted by color or patterns. Give this picture a try and see how you do with it.

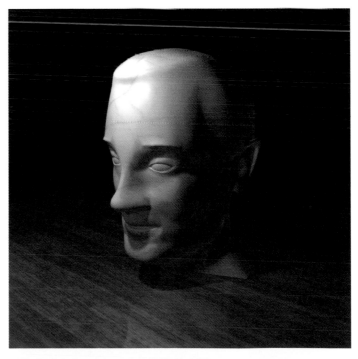

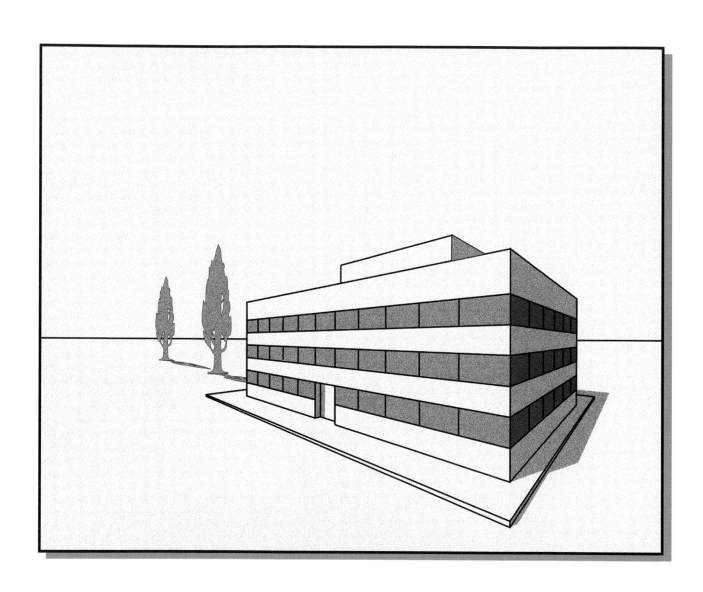

5

Gaining Perspective

Perspective is a way of perceiving things. Phrases such as, "Take a step back and gain some perspective," or "If you had a little more perspective on the problem, you might see the answer," are common. The term "gaining perspective" has come to mean looking at the big picture, seeing things from a broader view. It has also come to mean putting things where they belong in relation to each other. In many ways, perspective in art means putting things where they belong in a picture.

Perspective is an artistic term used to describe how artists create flat drawings that appear to be three-dimensional. Perspective is all about representing elements in a drawing so that they are accurately represented as three-dimensional using a system of lines connected to one or more vanishing points on a horizon line. It is an organization system for pictures.

Perspective

In the natural world items appear smaller the farther away they are from the viewer. For example, if someone is standing next to you, he will appear larger. If that same person were to walk away from you, he would appear to decrease in size. When an artist draws a scene, objects and characters need to be sized so that they are correct in relation to other objects or characters in the scene, but this isn't always easy for artists. Even simple objects can be difficult to visualize properly without some way of understanding special relationships.

To assist artists in creating accurate depictions of three-dimensional spaces, a system of organizing picture elements called *linear perspective* was developed during the early years of the Renaissance.

Linear Perspective

In the early days of the Renaissance, a young artist by the name of Giotto di Bondone revolutionized the art world by depicting characters and scenes that appeared three-dimensional. Prior to that time, Byzantine and Gothic art were primarily flat. Giotto's art was different, and he is often credited with beginning the Italian Renaissance.

From Giotto's early explorations of three-dimensional space on flat surfaces, artists refined a system of drawing that forms the basis for linear perspective as taught today in art classes around the world.

Linear perspective is the process of using lines drawn from a vanishing point on the horizon to organize and place elements in a drawing so that they appear correctly to the viewer. To understand how linear perspective works, first you need to understand the concept of a horizon line.

Horizon Line

A *horizon line* is where the ground meets the sky. Here, the darker brown area on the bottom represents the ground; the lighter blue on the top represents the sky. The black line where the two meet is the horizon line.

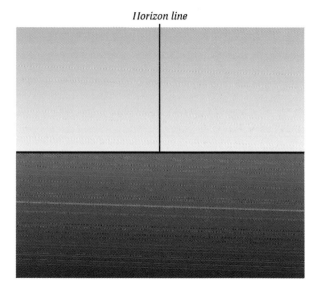

Horizon line

If you were to picture the world extending out in a flat plane from where you stand, the line where the plane meets the sky is the horizon line. This is very important to understand because sometimes mountains or buildings might obscure the horizon line.

The horizon line forms the basis for linear perspective. It changes depending on the angle that is used in the picture. If you look up, the horizon line goes down. For example, viewing a plane in the air requires you to look at the sky.

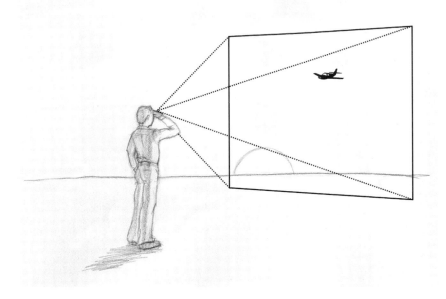

On the other hand, if you shift your view lower to see a motorcycle, the horizon moves up in the picture frame.

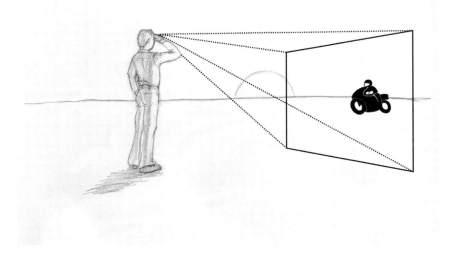

When objects in the scene, such as mountains or buildings, obscure the horizon line, the artist has to determine where the horizon line is based on the view. Here, the horizon line is estimated because the buildings are blocking a clear view of the horizon.

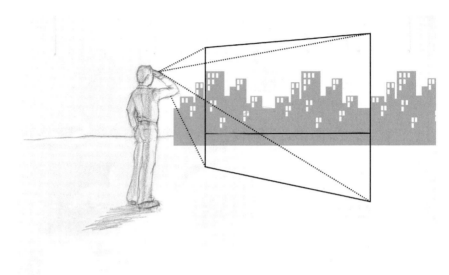

Vanishing Point

Another concept that is important to linear perspective is the vanishing point. A *vanishing point* is a point on the horizon that an object or character recedes to. A good example is to imagine standing in the middle of a straight road. The point at which the road meets the sky is the vanishing point.

In this example only one vanishing point is used. This is termed *single-point perspective* because all the objects in the picture are receding to a single vanishing point. Single-point perspective is the most basic form of linear perspective.

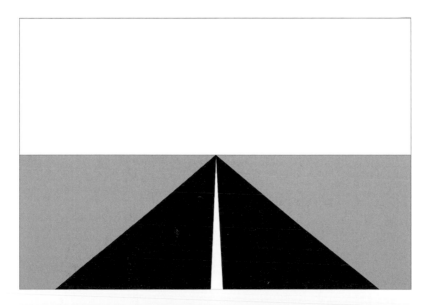

Vanishing Point

Even if the object does not extend to the horizon, it will still recede to a single point. The fundamental principle is that parallel lines will recede to a single point on the horizon line. The cube here shows a line projected along the parallel edges converging on a single point on the horizon line.

You might also notice that the cube's reflection and shadow also recede to the same vanishing point. Reflections will always recede to the same vanishing point as the object. Shadows in sunlight will also recede to the same vanishing point as the object; however, this only works in sunlight where the light rays travel so far from the sun that they are almost exactly parallel by the time they reach the Earth. Shadows don't follow this rule for most manmade light.

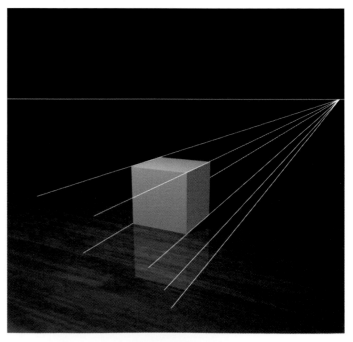

Two-Point Perspective

The most common type of linear perspective is two-point perspective. In two-point perspective, objects are defined by two separate vanishing points. Here you can see how two-point perspective applies to the cube.

Notice that in order to find the vanishing point for the other side of the cube, the horizon line had to be extended beyond the picture. This is often the case with drawings. Often one or more vanishing points extends beyond the picture frame.

The vanishing points help the artist to construct an accurate picture. Sometimes these vanishing points extend off the page quite a distance. If one of them is missing, the picture will easily become distorted because the artist will have no guidance while drawing. I often find many problems, whether in art or anything else, have vanishing points that extend off the picture or are outside the situation. For example, a boy who suddenly becomes disruptive and mean to his classmates viewed in the isolation of the classroom might be labeled as a problem student. However, viewed from a larger perspective, the teacher might find that the boy's parents are getting a divorce and the boy is really a frightened child.

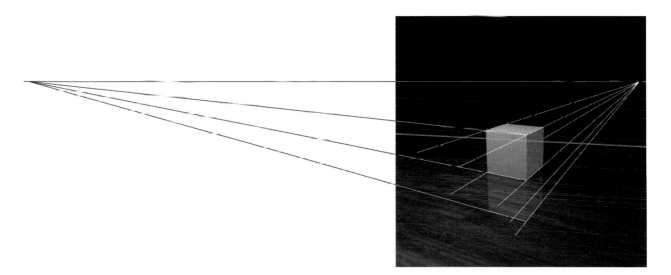

Two-point perspective adds to the realism of a picture because it allows for two sides of the object to recede from view. With two-point perspective, the additional vanishing point makes it possible for the artist to draw an object from any angle. This figure shows two cubes, one lower than the horizon line and one higher than the horizon line.

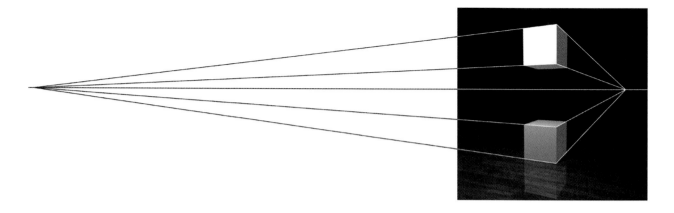

All objects in a picture are not always oriented to the same vanishing points. If the picture is of a city street, the buildings might line up with a similar or the same vanishing point, but other objects in the scene will most likely not. By changing the vanishing points for the objects in a scene, the artist is able to change their orientation to the viewer. Here you can see two cubes with different vanishing points. See whether you can find the vanishing points for each cube.

Three-Point Perspective

Two-point perspective will be adequate for the artist in most situations, but some situations will require even more accuracy. Notice that in two-point perspective, all of the vertical lines are parallel to each other. This isn't very noticeable to us because often the convergences of these lines are so distant that most of the time we don't notice the difference.

Some objects are so massive that they will look odd with only two-point perspective. In addition, extreme visual angles often call for more than a two-point approach. That is where three-point linear perspective comes into play. With the addition of a third point not connected to the horizon line, the artist is able to have the object recede from view correctly. Here you can see how three-point perspective works: The cube seems more massive with the addition of a third point.

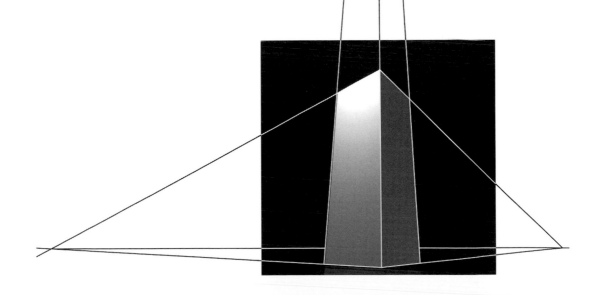

Often the third point is some distance from the picture. Finding the third point is easy. Suppose you are drawing a building.

1 Start your drawing by putting in a horizon line and two vanishing points, one on either side of your paper.

2 Now draw two lines—one from each vanishing point—so that they intersect toward the bottom center of the paper.

3 Draw another line extending up vertically from the intersection of the two lines.

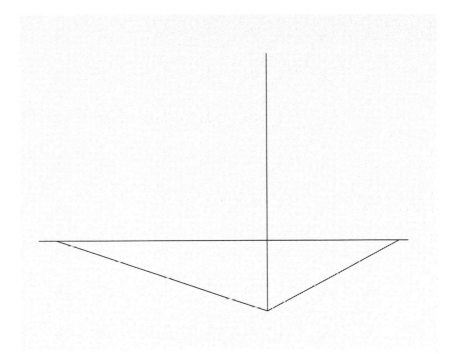

4 Now draw two more lines, one originating from each vanishing point, intersecting on the vertical line to form the top of the cube.

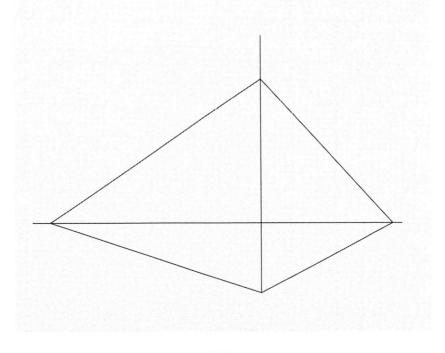

5 Establish a third vanishing point along the vertical line, well above the top of the cube.

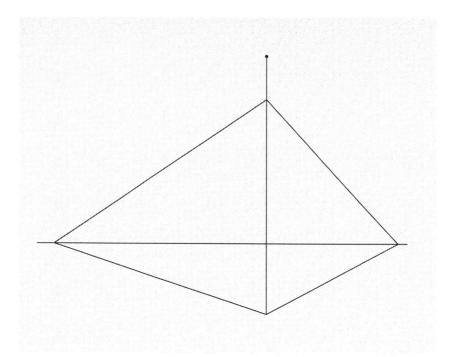

6 From the third vanishing point, draw a line down to the bottom construction line on the right side of the paper to define the right side of the building.

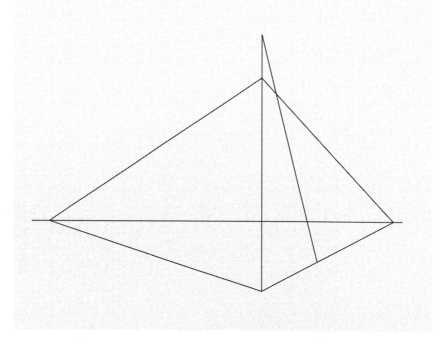

7 Now draw another line down the left side of the cube to establish the left side of the building.

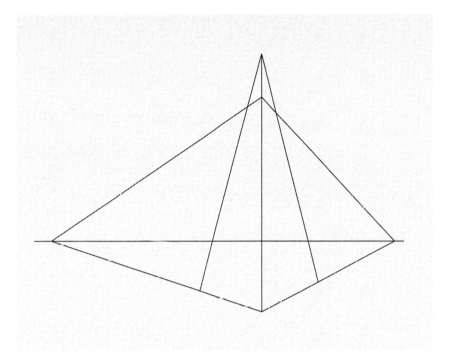

8 Now all you have to do is color in the building as shown here.

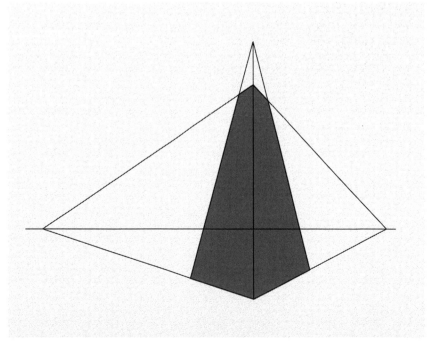

Drawing with Perspective

Now that you have gone over linear perspective a little, are you ready to try some drawing? Get a fresh sheet of paper and a straight edge that is long enough to match your paper.

You will be drawing an office building using two-point perspective. It will be a simple building, but it should give you a good understanding of how linear perspective works to create objects in a scene.

1 First draw a horizon line about one-third of the way up the paper, as shown in the figure at the top of this page.

2 Next draw some construction lines for the bottom of the building. Make sure you draw the perspective construction lines lightly so they can be erased later.

3 Draw a vertical line extending up from the intersection of the construction lines that form the base of the building.

4 The vertical line will be the corner of the building closest to the viewer. From the top of the vertical line, draw a line back to the right-hand vanishing point, as shown here.

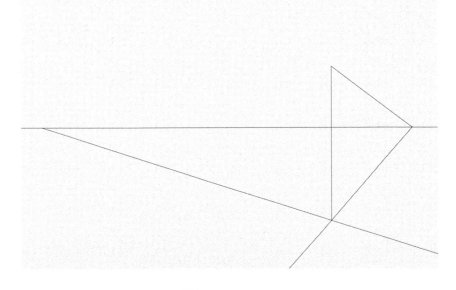

5 Now draw a line extending from the top of the vertical line to the left-hand vanishing point. These two top lines will define the roof of the building.

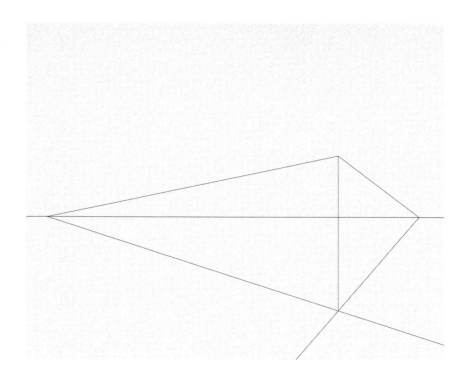

6 Draw two more vertical lines, as shown here. These lines define the right and left corners of the building.

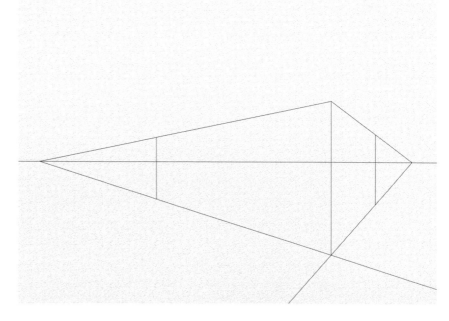

7 Just for fun, draw lines extending from the sides of the building back to the opposite vanishing points. These construction lines show where the back of the building should be. A vertical line where these lines intersect shows the fourth corner of the building.

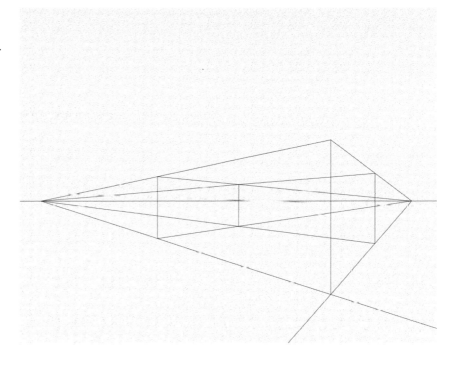

8 With darker lines, define the actual shape of the building following the construction lines already in place on the drawing.

9 To avoid confusion, erase all of the construction lines for the back of the building. You no longer need construction lines, so you can erase them so your drawing doesn't get too complex. If you have drawn your construction lines lightly, erasing them should not be a problem.

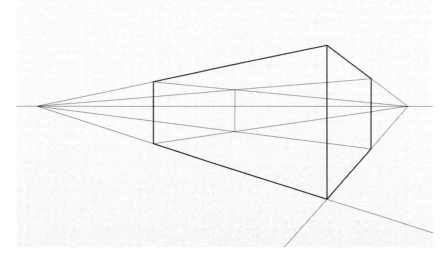

10 This will be a three-story office building. Next draw in the construction lines to define the windows of the building, as shown here.

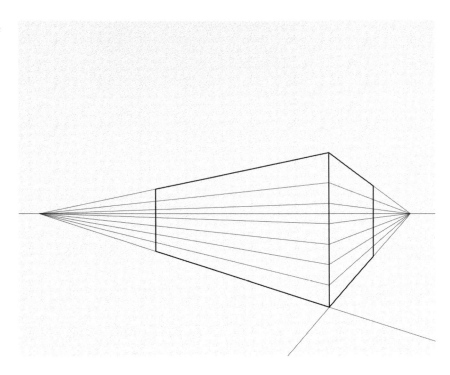

11 Draw in heavier lines for the windows and erase the now-unnecessary window construction lines.

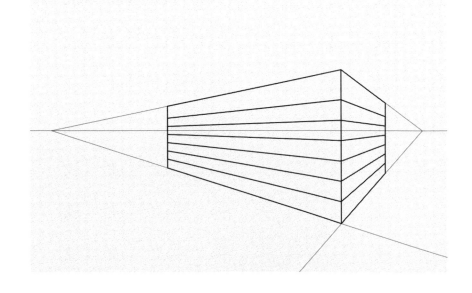

12 Now for the individual windowpanes. First, on the left side of the building, define one of the windows with a vertical line, as shown here.

13 Because all of the windows are the same size and on the same plane, they will recede evenly. There is a simple way to define how evenly spaced elements can recede from the viewer. Here is how it is done. First you need to find the center of the windows. To find the center, draw two lines from the corners of the window, intersecting in the middle.

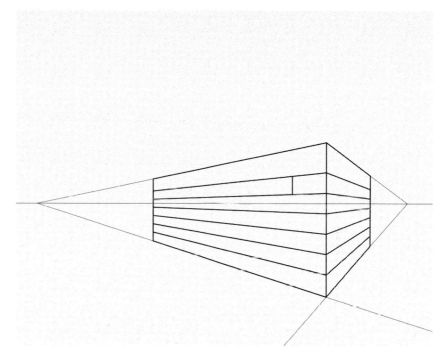

14 Now draw a line from the left vanishing point to the intersection of the crossed lines on the window. This new line defines the vertical center of the row of windows.

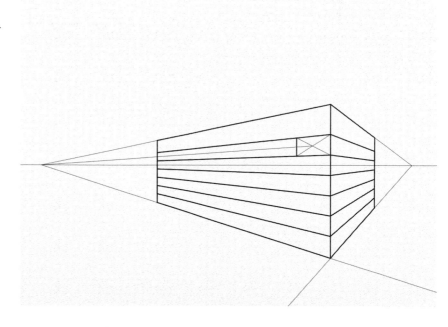

15 From the top-right side of the established window, draw a line that intersects the left side of the window at the point where it crosses the center line. Extend the line to the bottom of the row of windows. The end of the next window will be where the line intersects with the bottom of the row.

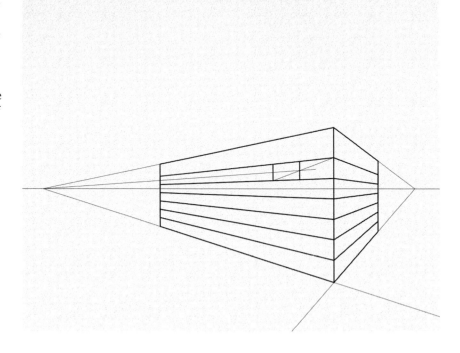

16 Use the same method to find the next window, and continue doing this all the way down the left side of the building.

17 Now define the top row of windows along the right side of the building in the same way that you did the left side. Make the windows narrower because the right side is receding more sharply than the left side.

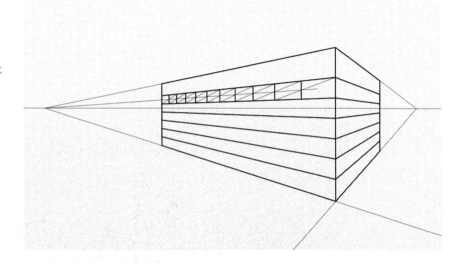

18 The windows in the rows below the top will be the same size as the top row of windows. You can draw them in using the top windows as a guide.

19 The building needs an entrance. Count the windows on the bottom row and find the middle window. Erase the bottom line of the window and extend the sides of the window down to the base of the building. This will be the doorway.

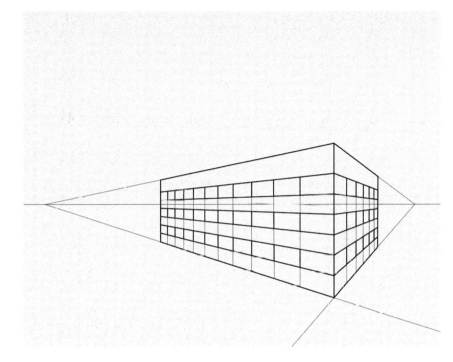

20 Now use the vanishing points to recess the door into the side of the building, as shown here.

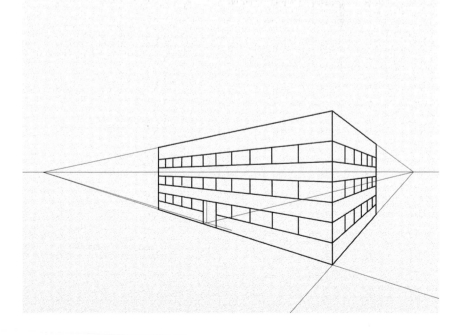

21 Use the vanishing points to put in a sidewalk around the building.

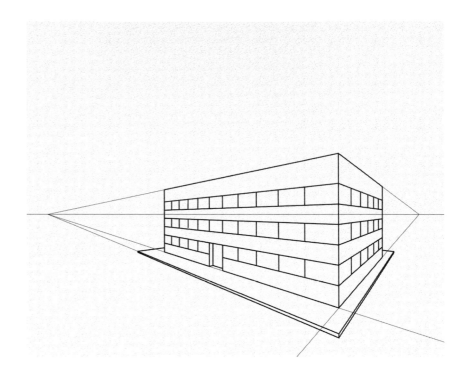

22 When you have objects that are roughly the same size, such as trees, you can use linear perspective to place the objects in the scene. Here, I placed two trees by the building. Notice how the use of linear perspective gives me a guide for the placement and size of the trees. I also added a small structure on top of the roof.

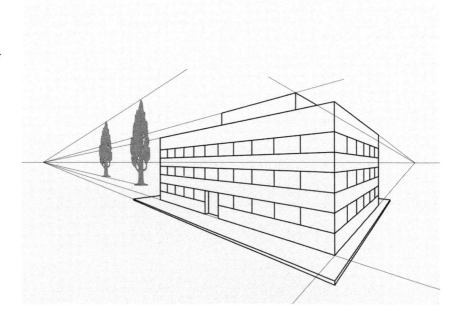

23 Now you can add some shadows to your scene with the help of linear perspective. Draw a line extending from the top-right corner of the building to the ground at the angle of the sun. Then draw a second line parallel to the first from the top front corner.

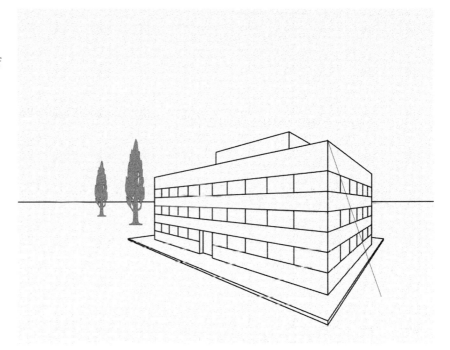

24 Next, draw a line from the vanishing point to intersect both of the lines from the roof, as shown here.

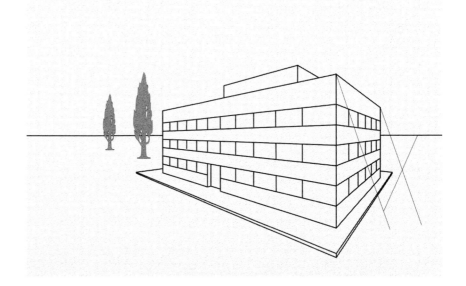

25 Now draw two lines from the intersection of the lines, the back intersection going to the left vanishing point and the front intersection going to the lower corner of the building.

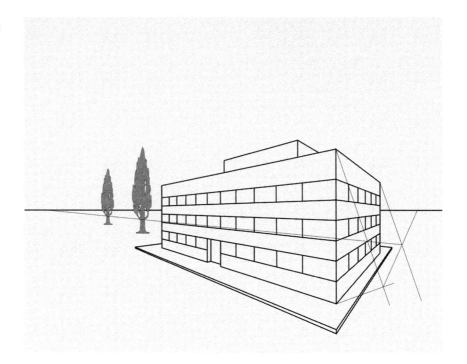

26 You now need to account for the sidewalk with the shadow, as shown here.

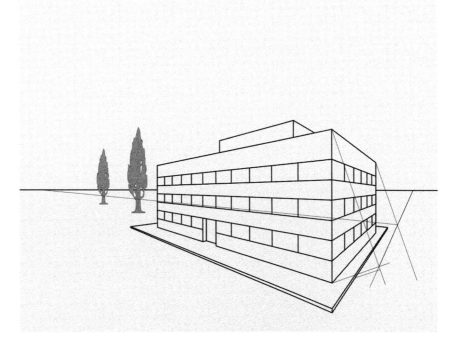

27 Use the construction lines as guides to add shadows to the drawing.

As you can see, linear perspective can be used in a number of ways to draw almost anything. Whenever you are drawing, you should always keep in mind linear perspective and use it to help organize the elements of your drawings.

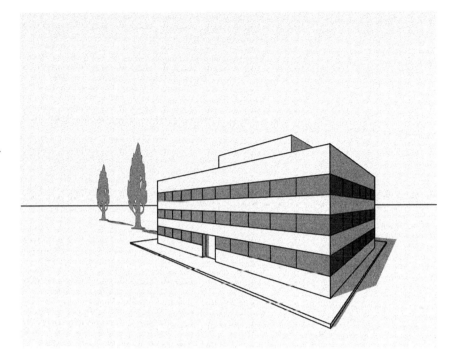

A great way to better understand linear perspective is to try finding it in photographs. Here you can see a photo of a parking lot, and below it an overlay showing the perspective lines. Try finding linear perspective in a few of your own photographs.

Aerial Perspective

In addition to linear perspective, there is another type of perspective that you should be aware of. It is called *aerial perspective*. Aerial perspective is the tendency of things to lose contrast as they recede from the viewer.

Air is not always clear. In fact, even on a clear day our view of distant objects is partially obscured by fine particles that float in the air. On foggy days our view might be completely blocked. Indicating this effect in art is called *aerial perspective*. Depending on the distance and the amount of haze in the air, objects become less distinct. Here you can see the effects of aerial perspective in nature. Notice that

the flowers in the foreground are clear and sharp, and the mountains in the distance are more in the mid tones.

Reducing the contrast and detail in distant objects gives the appearance that they are more distant than objects that have higher contrast and greater detail.

Now that you understand how to use perspective, try drawing a few scenes around your home. You might even try drawing your house or apartment building. As you get better at drawing using perspective, you will gain a lot of confidence in drawing manmade objects, such as buildings and roads.

6

Composition

Composition is a term used in art to describe how a picture is designed. Compositions can be good or bad. The can be dynamic or stately. When done right, a composition can make an otherwise dull subject interesting. When done poorly, a composition can make an otherwise interesting subject boring. This chapter will cover methods of creating good compositions.

Composition is related to perspective in that it is also a way of organizing a picture. But whereas perspective deals with how things are organized based on how they appear in three-dimensional spaces, composition deals with how the elements of a picture are arranged within the picture.

For someone who is new to art, composition might seem like a mystery, but like organizing anything, from your taxes to your daily schedule, organizing a picture is understandable if you know a few fundamental principles.

- ▶ **Purpose**
- ▶ **Placement**
- ▶ **Balance**
- ▶ **Focal points**
- ▶ **Pathways**

In many ways, organizing a picture is similar to organizing your daily schedule. First you have to lay out the reason or purpose for the planned activities. Next you have to place the activities within the available time. Each activity has to be balanced with all of the other activities. You must focus on important activities in order to complete them, and there must be clear avenues or pathways to go from one activity to another.

Purpose

Every drawing can and should have a purpose. The purpose might be as simple as seeing something interesting and drawing it. Or the purpose might be that the artist has a message or feeling that is expressed in the art.

In commercial art the purposes are almost always well-defined. The purpose is part of the assignment the artist is given. Sell this car. Convey this thought. Draw this building. Express this feeling. Draw attention to this product. All of these things are parts of the challenges for the commercial artist.

In fine art the need for a purpose is still there, but the artist generally determines what that purpose is. The purpose might be a feeling, such as serenity or excitement. It might be to capture the lighting of a scene, or it might be to express a personality in a portrait.

There really is no limit on the types of purposes for a drawing. One of the intrinsic values of art is that almost anything can be expressed through visual media. Often beginning artists will limit the scope of their expression to drawing or painting exactly what they see and never going beyond that to see what they express in their work. It is like living a life without direction: You never really get anywhere.

I once had an English professor who taught me an important lesson about art and life. At the beginning of the term a student asked him about the importance of spelling and grammar. His reply was that he didn't really care if there were a few mechanical mistakes in our work. He was more interested in whether or not we had anything to say. In other words, he wanted us to do what I call *meaningful writing*: He wanted our work to mean something. His feeling was that he would rather see a meaningful paper with a few mechanical errors than a well-crafted paper of meaningless prose.

My English professor's comments have always stuck with me, and I have tried applying his philosophy to most things in my life, including my art. I have found the best way to really have meaning is to start with a purpose. Define the purpose of the picture, and then develop the picture around that purpose.

So how do you develop purpose for a picture? The simple truth is that most pictures have a purpose, even if the picture is just a doodle while waiting for the train. The purpose of the doodle might have only been to explore some thoughts while relaxing. If, on the other hand, the doodles were small designs related to a product the artist was thinking about or they were pictures of a place the artist wanted to visit, the purpose of the doodles could be more than simple relaxation.

Take a minute and think about the purpose of a picture of a favorite pet. The purpose of the picture might be to show others what your pet looks like. However there could be more to that purpose. Maybe you not only want to show what your pet looks like, but you also want to show your pet's personality. Maybe your pet is playful and active. Instead of drawing your pet resting, it might be more meaningful to draw your pet at play.

A deeper meaning for a picture of your pet might be to somehow express your feelings about the pet. Maybe you have a deep emotional attachment to your pet and you want your picture to capture that attachment. What could you draw that would express your feelings though your art?

Can you see how having a purpose for a picture moves the drawing from a simple picture to a work of art? Many of the most famous pictures in the grandest museums are there not because the artist was a skilled painter, but rather because the art had meaning.

Placement

lacement is the arranging of pictorial elements within the picture frame. It is not merely the placement of objects; rather, it is the placement of all elements of drawing, including lines, planes, patterns, values, and objects. The artist has to be able to look at not only the subject of the drawing, but also the individual drawing elements, such as lines, contours, and values. The way each of these elements is placed in a picture determines a composition.

The beginning artist often gets too involved in the subject of the drawing, rather than dealing with the pictorial elements of the drawing. Think of the pictorial elements as the building blocks of the drawing. For example, here there are three shapes—a square, a circle, and a heart. One or more lines define each shape.

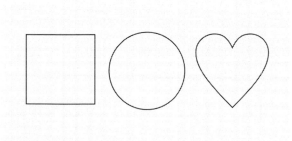

The quality and placement of the lines not only define the shape, they also define the picture. The picture is somewhat static because all of the lines are similar in weight and spacing. The shapes also are of equal size and centered on the paper.

By adjusting some of the drawing elements, you can see how the dynamics of the picture can change. Here, the shape of the circle was enlarged and the other two shapes were reduced. The circle is now the dominant shape. The dominant position of the circle is also enhanced by the fact that it is in the center of the picture.

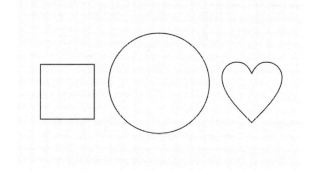

Here, the circle is moved to the side but the weight of the line is heavier, so even though it is not central, it is still dominant because of the heavier line.

The picture below is more interesting to look at than the first one because the lines in this one are dynamic. The lines are not one constant thickness; they vary widely from thick to thin. Just by changing the weight of the lines, the whole feel of the picture changes.

Another method of emphasizing a shape is to have it overlap the other shapes. The overlapping helps to increase the importance of the top shape and diminish the importance of the other two shapes. Here you can see the circle overlapping the other two shapes.

Value is also a drawing element, as shown below. The circle is darker than the other shapes. This contrast in value is one of the strongest drawing elements to emphasize a shape or element in drawing.

The way you place pictorial elements can have a big effect on the quality of your composition. For example, suppose you want to create a picture of your grandfather. A distinguishing feature of your grandfather is his smile. One method that you might try is designing your composition so that Grandpa's smile is in the center of the picture. You might also try lighting his face so that his eyes are in shadow while his smile is in full light.

Tangents

Sometimes the placement of objects can cause problems. For example, tangents can cause visual confusion. In this picture, the seal is supposed to be in the foreground. However, the placement of the seal's nose on the line of the barn gives the impression that the seal is balancing the barn on his nose.

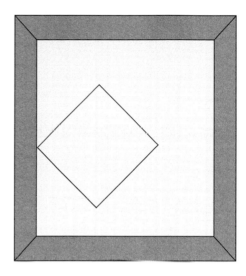

Tangents can also be painful. Here, the diamond shape is placed next to the edge of the picture.

When placing items in a picture, you should always watch out for potential problems with tangents that cause confusion in the placement of the visual elements in three-dimensional spaces.

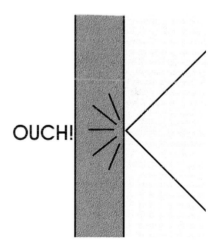

This causes two problems. First, the placement is uncomfortable because it is poking the side of the picture frame. It is almost like the frame is getting hurt! Second, sharp corners can often act as arrows, directing viewers' attention away from the picture.

Balance

Basic to composition is balance. If a picture is out of balance, it will feel uncomfortable to the viewer. In this picture, the character is way off to the right and facing away from the center of the picture. It creates a large, uncomfortable empty area in the middle and left side of the picture. The picture is off balance.

A good way to think of picture balance is to imagine that the picture is perched on triangle. If the picture feels like it would be heavier on one side than on another, the picture will seem off balance.

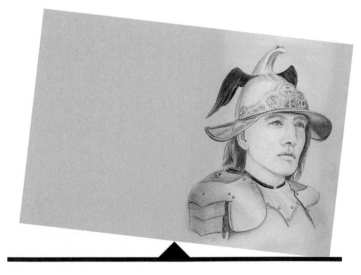

Granted, this illustration is exaggerated for purposes of this lesson. But even pictures that are just a little off balance can be uncomfortable. If a person is uncomfortable with a picture, he or she will tend to not enjoy looking at it and will probably move on to other pictures. I usually try to keep my pictures in balance unless I want to heighten the tension.

Formal Balance

One way to solve the balance problem is to use formal balance. *Formal balance* is a system of balancing a picture by subdividing it into equal portions so that one side mirrors the other. Formal balance feels comfortable to us because many things in life have symmetry. Most animals are symmetrical, as is the human body.

As a child, I remember getting a toy for a gift that had these little wheel-like gears that I could use to draw symmetrical designs. It was easy to draw very symmetrical designs using the gears for tools. I remember experimenting for hours to see the different types of designs that I could come up with. Here you can see a symmetrical design similar to the ones I made as a child. These symmetrical designs are pleasing to the viewer—almost beautiful—because most people like order and symmetry in their lives.

For compositions in which the artist wants to have a feeling of dignity or majesty, formal balance or symmetry is a great approach. Here is an example of how a picture can be subdivided to achieve a formal balance.

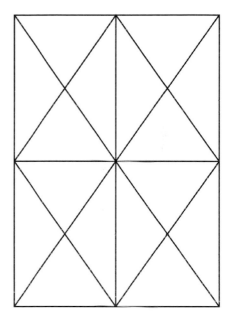

Not everything needs to be mirrored from one side to the other, but there should be a sense of equality in the masses from one side to the other for a picture to have formal balance.

Leonardo da Vinci (1452-1519). The Annunciation. 1618.
Erich Lessing/Art Resource, NY

Many of the great masters used formal balance in their painting. Take a look at some of these famous pictures for examples of formal balance.

In the high Renaissance, formal balance was a widely used system for picture composition. Leonardo da Vinci was a master of formal balance, as shown here.

Leonardo da Vinci (1452-1519).
Mona Lisa. Réunion des Musées
Nationaux/Art Resource, NY

Other contemporaries of da Vinci also used formal balance. These two examples are from Michelangelo and a later artist by the name of Tintoretto.

Formal balance is great for formal pictures, but because it is so balanced the pictures can sometimes lack dynamics. Formal balance is not very good for creating pictures that give the feeling of motion or action. The artist needs to have other ways to balance a picture.

Tintoretto, Jacopo Robusti (1518-1594). Miracle of Saint Mark. 1548. Scala/Art Resource, NY

Michelangelo (1475-1564). Holy Family. Scala/Art Resource, NY

Informal Balance

Objects or characters in a composition don't have to be equal in size or mass to balance a picture. Artists can use the principle of the fulcrum lever in compositions to create a feeling of balance even though the objects are two different sizes. A fulcrum lever is like a teeter-totter, as shown here.

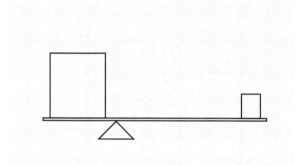

The center of the teeter-totter is the fulcrum. A heavier person can teeter-totter with a lighter person by moving closer to the fulcrum or having the lighter person move farther away from the fulcrum. By placing a larger object or character near the center of the picture and placing the smaller object farther from the center, the picture will have a sense of balance. This approach to balance can add more drama to a picture.

This picture uses this method to balance the character in the foreground with the castle in the distance.

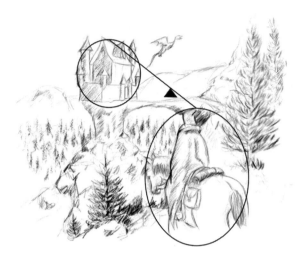

The pictures on the next page show examples of the fulcrum-lever approach to balance in some famous paintings by masters of the northern Renaissance, Rembrandt van Rijn and Pieter Pauwel Rubens. Rembrandt used informal balance to create many of his paintings.

As with most things, balance is important. If our lives get out of balance, things start falling apart. Balance keeps a picture cohesive, just as it keeps a life cohesive. Have you ever known someone who is obsessed with something? How was their life? Were they uncomfortable to be around?

Although it is often good to be focused on things, without balance we can lose perspective on our lives. Learning to balance a picture is similar to learning to balance other things in our lives. Like placing things in a picture so that one side doesn't feel heavier than the other, we can place things in life so that we maintain a balance and avoid obsessions.

Rembrandt Harmensz van Rijn (1606-1669).
Self-portrait as a young man. Alinari/Art
Resource, NY

Rembrandt Harmensz van Rijn (1606-1669). The Woman taken into
Adultery. 1644. Art Resource, NY

Rubens, Peter Paul (1577-1640). Self-Portrait,
1638-40. Erich Lessing/Art Resource, NY

Focal Points

Have you ever noticed that while looking at a picture, your eyes tend to be drawn to a specific area? It's almost like that part of the picture is screaming, "Hey! Look at me first!" That doesn't always happen by accident. In fact, many artists spend a great deal of time planning how you will view their picture. They create focal points and pathways in their work.

A *focal point* is an area in the picture that calls for attention. The call can be blatant, like a noisy child in a quiet classroom, or it can be gentle, like a bubbling brook in the mountains.

In many pictures there is more than one focal point. The artist builds a chain of two or more focal points, with the major focal point demanding the most attention and each succeeding focal point diminishing in importance. A picture with two equally demanding focal points can be frustrating to the viewer.

Focal points in art and life are similar. In art, a focal point is something that draws attention. In life, a focal point can be something that we excel in or something that is important to us, such as a particular cause or our religion.

Life gives us many opportunities to attract the attention of others. They happen to all of us. Maybe you have a business presentation or some other public-speaking engagement. You might be a teacher in a school or some other organization. Maybe you are a business owner looking for a way to attract consumer attention to your business. Or maybe it's more personal. You just feel lonely and ignored and want someone to take some interest in you. Whatever it is, the idea of creating focal points in life is important.

I remember talking to a young lady one time who was very down on herself. She felt that she was unattractive and unappealing. As an artist, I tend to notice beauty in almost everyone. This young lady had dark, beautiful hair. As we talked, I mentioned that her hair was quite beautiful. I suggested that she make her hair a focal point. She took my suggestion and started wearing her hair down, instead of pulling it back as she often had. Not only did her beautiful hair get noticed, she started feeling better about herself. I am sure that there was a lot more to her loneliness than changing a hairstyle, but just that one little thing had an effect on her life.

Just like in the case of the young lady's hair, artists can highlight things in their art that might otherwise go unnoticed. Museums are full of pictures of mundane things that become interesting because the artist knew how to create a focal point on the scene that was unique to his or her vision. In the picture here, Rembrandt focused the attention on the helmet rather than the person by the way he used light to illuminate the painting.

Rembrandt Harmensz van Rijn (1606-1669). Man with the Golden Helmet. Bildarchiv Preussischer Kulturbesitz/Art Resource, NY

Linear Focus

One of the most effective methods of creating a focal point is to use the lines in the picture to point to the focus point. This is called *linear focus* and it is derived from the viewer's tendency to not view lines or edges as static images. When viewing a picture, your eyes will tend to slide along a line. If many of the lines converge on a single point or area of the picture, a focal point is created. In this picture, you can see how the lines of the picture converge on the castle, making it the focal point of the picture. The overlaid lines indicate the general direction of the elements.

Contrast Focus

Another excellent way to create a focal point is to use value contrast. *Value* is the quality of light or dark in a picture. In this picture, the focal point is the silhouette of the knight on horseback. Notice how quickly your eyes are drawn to the focal area. Contrast focus in static pictures is more likely to catch the viewer's eye than any other focus method is.

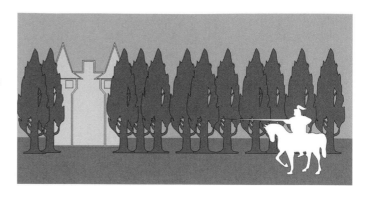

To create a focal point using value, the artist places the highest contrast between light and dark at the focal point. All other images in the picture will have less contrast between light and dark.

Here you can see a more subtle use of contrast focus. Notice how the greatest contrast in value is in the girl's eyes. The eyes demand that the viewer pay attention to them.

Detail Focus

Detail in a picture will create a focal point. The eye is naturally drawn to areas of the picture that have greater detail. This is a simple picture made up of mostly flat shapes. By adding a few lines of definition to the bicycle rider, the eye is naturally drawn to him, creating a focal point.

Color Focus

Another very effective way to create a focal point is to use color. In this picture, the background is made of colors comprising variations from blue to red. The trophy is a bright yellow opposite the background colors on the color wheel. It is the only color in the yellow family in the picture, causing the viewer's eye to focus on it.

Action Focus

Action and movement are very strong attention devices that are often used in motion pictures, video games, and the Internet. Because drawings don't generally move, the application of action as a focal point is somewhat difficult. Instead of having something move in the drawing, the artist has to imply movement. *Implied movement* is movement that is about to happen, such as when you capture a dynamic moment during a dramatic action. Here is an example of impending action. The polo player is about to strike the ball, creating interest in the scene.

Impending action is a powerful attention-grabber. If the subject in a picture looks like he is about to do something, it naturally calls us to look to see what he is about to do.

Most of the these examples are extreme to illustrate the different ways that lines, value, detail, color, and action can be used to focus the viewer's attention on a point in the picture. In practice, the artist should use judgment in the methods used to focus attention. The danger in being too heavy-handed with compositions is that when any technique or method of composition becomes too overbearing, the viewer can feel manipulated. Composition techniques should be used in such a way that they seem natural to the viewer, not contrived.

Pathways

Sometimes, rather than a single focal point in a picture, the artist might want to have a series of focal points connected by pathways. A *pathway* is usually a linear or value pictorial element that connects one focal point to another. Here you can see a blatant pathway between the shapes in the picture. The curved line connects them.

While this picture does illustrate the concept of visual pathways, it is a little overbearing and contrived. A more challenging concept for the artist is to build pathways that seem natural to the viewer. Here, pathways are part of the elements of the picture. One of the natural pathways is shown with the black line. See whether you can find a few others.

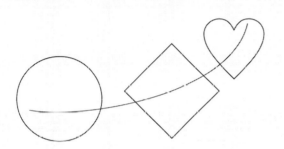

If there are natural pathways in the picture, the viewer will be able to comfortably scan the picture, moving from focal point to focal point. If the picture lacks natural pathways, it will feel uncomfortable to the viewer, causing tension. Here you can see a painting by Pieter Pauwel Rubens. Though this is a simple portrait, Rubens still paid attention to the visual pathways in the picture. The way the figure has her hands folded and the position of her hat combine to create a natural pathway for the eyes to follow.

You have just covered a number of composition concepts in a single chapter. I hope that composition is not such a mystery for you now. A very good way to test yourself is to take an art history book and see whether you can find some of the concepts covered here in the art that you find in it.

Try drawing a few pictures using a few concepts from this chapter. Don't worry about getting everything into a single picture; just try them one at a time. As you get more familiar with these concepts, you will be able to start using them in your work to add more meaning and purpose to what you do.

Rubens, Peter Paul (1577-1640). Portrait of Suzanne Fourment. Erich Lessing/Art Resource, NY

7

Seeing and Drawing People

Finally, at Chapter 7 we come to one of my favorite subjects to draw—people. I find drawing people both fascinating and challenging. People are fascinating because we come in so many shapes and sizes and have so many different characteristics, such as ethnic and cultural differences. Yet with all the differences we are still very much alike. Most people have two eyes, walk on two legs, and talk with one mouth. It is hard to imagine any subject so similar yet so individual at the same time.

The human form transcends the history of art from the earliest cave paintings to the present time. Our fascination with ourselves has led to some of the greatest masterpieces ever created. Great masters such as Rembrandt, da Vinci, Michelangelo, Velasquez, Rubens, David, Picasso, and more have all focused on the human figure in their work.

One of the reasons for the abundance of figurative art is the amazing range of emotional potential with humans as subjects. We cry. We smile. We laugh. We cheer. No other subject has the potential for emotional diversity that comes packaged in one person.

Many beginning artists avoid drawing people because the stakes are just too high. I have known several professional artists who are so intimidated by drawing a person that they will avoid it at all costs. They focus their energy on other subjects, such as buildings, landscapes, or cartoons. Although they might not have to deal with drawing people in their professional career, they miss out on one of the most enjoyable aspects of drawing.

In all of the subjects that you want to draw, are people included? Do you have an interest in drawing your loved ones? If you have tried to draw people before and didn't like what you drew, it is probably because you didn't understand your subject well enough. If you want to draw people well, you have to begin by learning how to see people.

Seeing People

As humans we are relatively familiar with ourselves. I believe that this familiarity is one of the biggest reasons why drawing a person is likely the most intimidating subject that an artist can approach—that and the fact that we are also very complex. I also believe that a person is one of the most fascinating subjects for artists to draw.

Familiarity with ourselves both helps and hinders the artist in learning how to draw people. It helps because the artist already knows the subject. It hinders because the artist assumes an understanding of the subject and draws without really looking at it.

Let me give a quick example. Often one of the most glaring errors that beginning artists make is to draw a person with the features of the face too high on the head. The artist assumes that because there is so much going on between the eyes and the chin and so little between the eyes and the top of the head, the features of the face should take up most of the room on the head. The fact is that a normal human head has the eyes about halfway between the top of the head and the bottom of the chin, as shown here.

There are many other aspects of the human form that you might not have noticed. In this chapter I will help you with many of them, but not all of them can be covered in one chapter. This chapter, like this book, is a starting point. It is just the launching pad for the beginning artist to start exploring. My hope is that you will follow this book with more artistic training.

Learning to draw means learning to draw anything and everything you want to draw and not hiding from more difficult subjects. The difficulty in drawing people comes from how well we know ourselves. When you are drawing a tree, if you move a branch up or down a few feet very few people will notice the difference. On the other hand, if you move a feature on someone's face even just a few millimeters, almost everyone will notice that something is wrong. Take a look at the two pictures here. Do you see a problem with one of the faces? The eyes in the second picture are not even, giving the portrait an uncomfortable feeling.

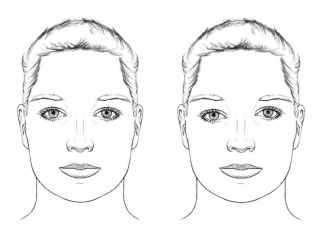

Drawing people requires a great deal more accuracy than drawing other subjects. It also requires a lot more feeling than other types of drawing do. The problem is compounded by the fact that human figures are organic, so drawing aides such as rulers are useless. But even with all of the challenges, there are still many aspects of the human form that an artist can learn to help with drawing people.

Proportion

Proportion in figure drawing is a term used to describe accurately defining relative distances between physical features of the human body. This means that when you are drawing people, all aspects of the body are related to each other so that no part is drawn too small or too large.

Proportions of the Head

Let's start looking at proportion with the head. This drawing of a head shows the front and the side.

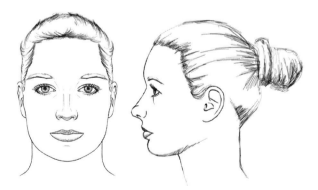

Although there are individual variations, most heads fall within some general guidelines.

▶ **The face can be divided into four horizontal sections. The hairline is in the top section. The top of the eyes and eyebrows are in the next quarter section. The bottom of the eyes and the nose are in the next lower quarter, and the mouth and chin are in the bottom quarter.**

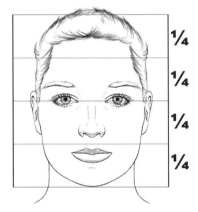

▶ **The distance between the eyes is about one eye-width, as shown here. Notice that the nose is also about an eye-width wide. Noses vary in width quite a bit, so this is not always the case.**

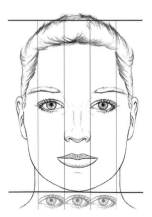

▶ The width of the mouth generally falls inside the distance between the pupils of the eyes, as shown here.

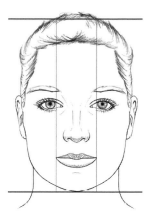

▶ The ears usually are as high as the top of the eyes and extend to near the bottom of the nose, as you can see here.

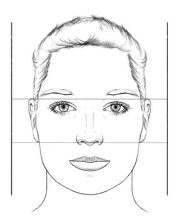

▶ The ears usually fall in the back half of the head, as seen from the side.

▶ When measuring from the tip of the nose to the back of the head, the base of the front of the neck falls at about the mid-point, as shown here.

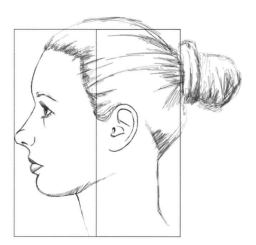

Construction Guide for the Head

With these principles in mind, you can now create a construction guide for drawing portraits. To help them accurately draw in 3D space, artists use construction guides as a framework for placing features.

Here is how it works: First, start with a circle. The circle will act as a guide for most of the skull. The bottom of the circle will generally fall somewhere between the mouth and the nose, and most of the time it will come to just below the cheekbones, as shown here.

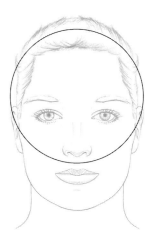

Notice that the circle extends out from the head on either side, past the ears. This is because the head is not a perfect circle. When drawing, you need to remember to bring the sides of the head inside the circle.

Split the circle in half both vertically and horizontally. The head is fundamentally symmetrical. The vertical line defines the center of the face. The horizontal line is used as a guide for placing features.

Once you have established the circle, draw in the jaw line. It will extend down below the circle, as shown here. Extend the vertical line to the bottom of the jaw.

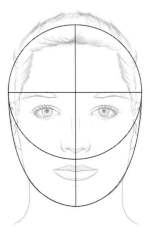

Divide the head construction with horizontal lines for the eyes, nose, and mouth, as shown here.

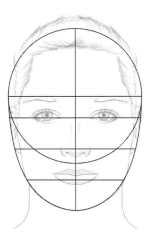

This is the basic construction guide for drawing a head from the front. In this image you can see the construction for drawing a head from the side.

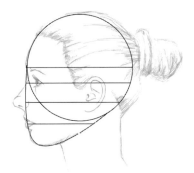

Not every head you draw will be a front view or a side view. Often the head will be turned to one side or the other or will be looking up or down. Most of the time, you will need to create the construction guide as a 3D shape. Here you can see the construction guide moved in a three-quarter turn with the circle, cross lines, and jaw line drawn in. Notice that the cross lines are drawn as ovals, indicating the turn of the head to the left and the tilting of the head slightly down.

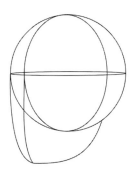

Next, draw in the lines defining the eyes, nose, and mouth, as shown here. The lines going around the back of the head are lightened so you can better see how they work.

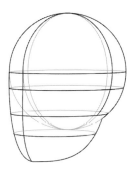

You can now use the lines to define the location of the features. Here you can see the construction guide over the face and the drawing when the guide is removed.

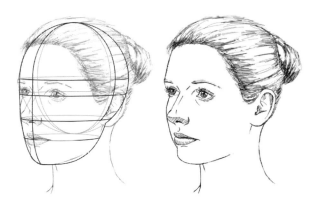

It takes a little practice to get the features in the right places using the construction guide. Remember that the construction guide defines the base of the nose where it protrudes from the face. The eyes, on the other hand, generally recess in from the line. The top cross line is just about the level of the eyebrows. The sides of the face do not extend all the way to the edge of the circle.

Try drawing a few faces on your own. Here is a construction guide that you can copy and use to practice with.

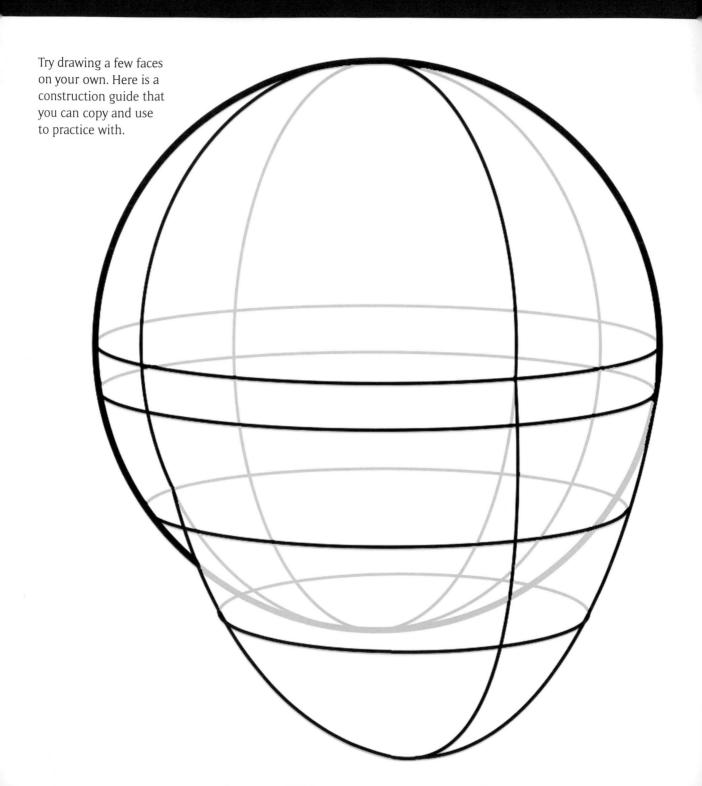

Drawing Portraits

A portrait is a picture of a specific individual. It is usually always a picture of the person's head, but sometimes it might include part or all of the person's body.

Drawing a portrait is a challenging task because people expect a portrait to look like the person being drawn. Having a portrait look like the subject of the drawing is called *creating a likeness* of the subject. To create a likeness, the artist has to be very careful in the construction of the face and very accurate in the shading and rendering.

In this example, I will show you how I created a portrait of Levi, a friend of mine. On the previous page you can see a photograph of Levi.

1 The first step is to look closely at the subject to pick up on anything that might be different than the standard construction for the head. When Levi smiles, he opens his mouth quite a bit. This causes his jaw to drop, making his chin lower. In addition, Levi's chin is longer than average. These two elements combine to set his eyes above the centerline.

2 After taking a long look at Levi's picture, draw in the basic construction guides modified to fit his head. Make sure that you draw very lightly, as shown here. The construction guide should be only dark enough that you can follow it—no darker. Keeping the construction guide light will help eliminate erasing later.

3 Once the construction guide is in place, use it to lightly draw in the basic shapes of each feature, as shown here. Remember, this is the planning stage of the drawing. Make sure you spend enough time on the construction of the face that you get everything as accurate as possible.

4 I usually start with the eyes because they tend to be the focal point of most of my portraits. In addition, the eyes usually have the biggest range from light to dark. By establishing the eyes first, I also establish the range of light to dark in the portrait. Here you can see some details in the area of the eyes as the drawing is developed.

5 From the eyes, next start to develop the nose and mouth areas. This is kind of an inside-out method to drawing portraits. Some artists like to work top to bottom, while other artists like to work a little in all areas. I like to work on the features of the face first, and then expand the drawing from there. Here you can see the progress of the drawing so far.

Hint

Glasses are usually a problem for portraits because of the glare on the glass and the distortion of the eyes. I usually draw the glasses as if there were no glass in the lenses because the highlight glare off the lenses is a harsh distraction from the person's face.

The problem with the distortion of the lenses is more an issue of how strong the prescription is. If the distortion is small, I draw the person as is, distortion and all. If the distortion is severe, it is better to draw the person without glasses and then add them later.

6 After the features of the face are shaded in, move on to the cheeks and chin areas and begin to shade them as well. The shading does not have to contain the full range of contrast at this point. The idea is to lightly define how the shading will work to define the contours of the face. In drawing it is better to err on the light side than the dark because you can always darken a picture, but in order to lighten one you must use an eraser, which has the potential to ruin the delicate fibers of the paper.

7 Continue down the face to the neck. The area under the chin is usually a darker area if the subject is lit from an overhead light.

8 The forehead and hair are next, including the ear.

9 Continue drawing outward until the neck and shoulders are drawn.

10 After the initial shading is defined, go back and darken the areas that are too light. Here you can see the portrait with a better dark-to-light ratio.

11 Finish the drawing by adding some background shading along the neck and cheeks to bring the face forward and give the head a more three-dimensional look, as shown here.

I hope your portrait turned out well for you. Now it's time to take a look at some of the individual features in a portrait.

Facial Features

I remember my first foundation drawing class in college. We were all freshman just beginning our coursework. Our art instructor was a seasoned artist with years of experience. When we came to the section on drawing people, he made us fill a sketchpad full of nothing but facial features. I drew pages of eyes and ears. I also drew mouths and noses. Part of the reason why he made us isolate each feature and draw it over and over again was that he wanted us to learn in detail how to draw each one. He also wanted us to get over the fear of drawing people. By isolating each feature, we were able to concentrate on only drawing one thing, and that was a lot less intimidating than drawing a full portrait.

Now you'll take a look at the individual features of the face and see how each one is drawn.

Eyes

The human eye is a spherical object recessed into the skull. We only see a part of it; it is covered by eyelids and protected by a ridge of bone that makes up the brow and cheekbones of the skull. Here you can see the many parts of the eye.

Following are some tips for drawing eyes:

- ▶ **Eyelids have thickness on the top and the bottom. It is most evident on the bottom lid.**
- ▶ **When drawing the lashes, plant the tip of the pencil at the base of each lash and release pressure on the pencil stroke as you draw in each lash.**
- ▶ **The highlights of the eye are direct reflections of the light source. This is always the brightest part of the eye—even brighter than the white of the eye.**
- ▶ **There is often a fold above the eye that becomes more evident the more the person opens his or her eyes.**
- ▶ **There is a cast shadow below the upper lid on the eyeball.**
- ▶ **Remember to draw the tear duct on the inner side of the eye.**
- ▶ **The pupil sits behind the lens of the eye, not on the surface of the eyeball.**
- ▶ **The eye bulges from the skull at the center because of its ball shape.**

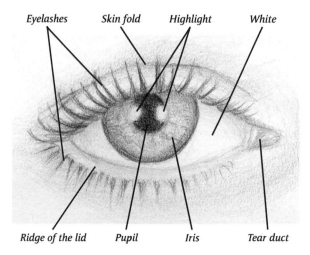

Eyelashes   *Skin fold*   *Highlight*   *White*

Ridge of the lid   *Pupil*   *Iris*   *Tear duct*

Nose

The nose is often one of the hardest features for a beginning artist to draw. That is because the nose is a protrusion from the face and is indicated mostly by delicate shading along the bridge. Often the beginning artist will try to draw the nose using lines from the eyes. It is better to think of the nose as a protruding structure that blends in with the other structures of the face, as shown here.

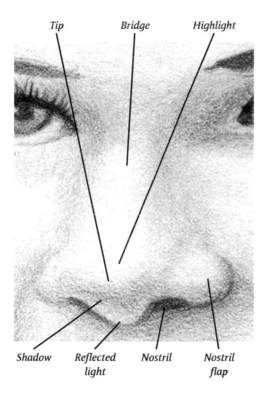

Tip   Bridge   Highlight

Shadow   Reflected   Nostril   Nostril
light   flap

A nose is made up of bone, cartilage, and soft tissue. The bony bump often seen on the ridge of adult male noses is the transition between the skeletal bone of the nose and the cartilage, as shown here. There are three pieces of cartilage in a nose, one along the bridge and then two at the tip of the nose. If you feel the tip of your nose with your finger, you should be able to sense the two plates and the small recess where they come together. With some noses, you can see this recess between the cartilage plates.

Both nostrils have a soft tissue flap that extends from the tip of the nose and around each nostril. The flap tucks into the upper lip and often forms a slight outward bulge.

The upper lip often reflects light to the lower part of the nose. The more ball-shaped the end of the nose is, the more this reflected light is evident.

The highlight of the nose is usually above the tip of the nose.

Noses are generally larger on older people because the nose continues to grow throughout our lives.

Mouth

The lips frame the mouth opening for the face, as shown here. They are primarily fleshy tissue with underlying muscles that enable movement. They form the most dominant feature of the mouth and are divided into two parts—the upper and lower lips.

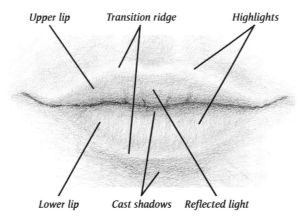

Upper lip   *Transition ridge*   *Highlights*

Lower lip   *Cast shadows*   *Reflected light*

The upper lip is attached to the skull, and the lower lip is attached to the jawbone. Because of the two separate bone attachments, the mouth has the widest range of change of any facial feature.

The lips cover the inner mouth and derive much of their shape from the teeth. If seen from one side or the other, there is a pronounced arch from the sides of the mouth to the middle, as shown here.

When you are drawing the mouth, the upper lip is usually in shadow from overhead lighting. The lower lip typically has more direct light and a highlight. The upper lip will often cast a shadow on the lower lip when the lips are together and on the teeth when they are apart.

There is a ridge of transition between the skin of the face and the flesh of the lips. This area is slightly lighter than the surrounding skin and is more noticeable on men and on people with darker flesh tones.

There is often a shadow beneath the lower lip above the chin. The larger the lower lip, the more likely the shadow will be evident.

When drawing the mouth open, draw the teeth as a single mass with shading. Come in later and define the individual teeth, as shown here. Remember that the teeth are generally in shadow even though they are white.

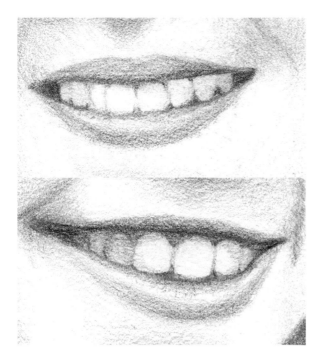

Ear

Ears vary widely in shape and size from person to person. Some people have large ears, and some people have small ears. Some ears lay flat against the skull, while others protrude. Older people tend to have larger ears than younger people because the ear continues to grow throughout our lives. Even though the ear is not prominently placed on the front of our faces, it is still a significant facial feature and should not be ignored.

The ear is basically a sound-catching mechanism and, as such, it acts as a funnel for sound waves. The fleshy outer parts of the ear channel sound to the concha, and then the inner ear through the ear canal. An anterior notch protects the ear canal from damage.

The ear is made up of a stiff yet flexible tissue that keeps its shape but can bend when needed. A ridge of skin called the *helix* surrounds the upper ear and the back of the ear. The lower part of the ear forms a lobe and is more flexible than the rest of the ear.

When drawing the ear, think of its many shapes and shade them according to the shading principles discussed earlier. There are many areas of cast shadow and reflected light. Most portraits view the ear from the front of the face, as shown here.

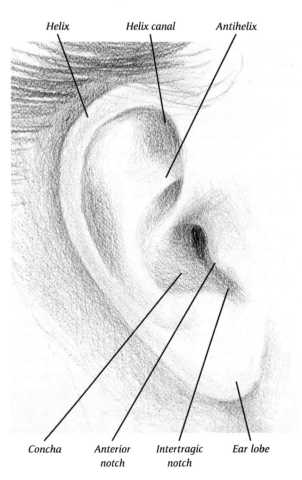

Helix   Helix canal   Antihelix

Concha   Anterior notch   Intertragic notch   Ear lobe

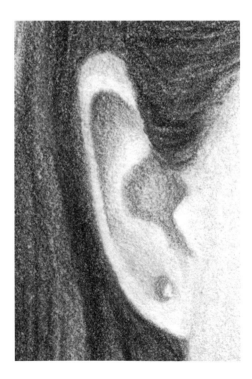

Hair

Hair is not an individual feature, such as a mouth or an eye; rather, it is made up of many separate strands. Often artists find hair difficult to draw because they don't understand how it catches light and how it flows.

Shadow area   Locks

Highlights   Transition areas

Hair is usually shiny and catches light with many highlights. It is usually a good idea to look at the highlights and shadow areas of hair first. The highlights will be the white of the paper unless the hair is very dark. Draw in the shadow areas first, and then draw in the transitional areas with individual pencil strokes emanating from the shadow areas toward the highlight areas. Each stroke should start dark and then lighten as pressure is released from the pencil.

Longer hair usually clumps in locks. A head of hair is made up of several overlapping locks. This is most evident in longer wavy or curly hair.

When the hair is parted, as shown here, there is usually a shadow area near the scalp and a highlight as the hair changes direction and lies against the skull.

As you can see, there are many facets to each facial feature in a portrait. I suggest that you spend some time working on each feature until you feel comfortable drawing it. Fill some sketchbooks with pictures of eyes, noses, mouths, ears, and hair. When you feel you've mastered the individual features, try putting them together in a complete portrait.

The Figure

Drawing people is not just drawing a person's head; there is an entire body as well to draw. In art, drawing a full figure of a person is called *figure drawing*. Drawing the human figure is a rewarding and demanding discipline. Entire books are devoted to it. In this chapter I will only touch on some of the basics to give you a start. Further study beyond this book will be necessary if you want to master the art of figure drawing.

Proportions of the Body

Body proportions vary widely in people, depending on whether the person is short or tall, fat or skinny, heavy or light boned, and so on. Rather than covering all of the differences, which would take more room than I have in this chapter, I will just cover basic proportions for an average person of average height and build.

Here you can see an outline of a male figure from the front and side. An average male figure is roughly seven and a half heads high. The midpoint for the figure intersects the hips and buttocks.

Note

When measuring a figure, artists often use some readily available unit of measurement. Because the head is easy to distinguish and rarely changes shape, it is a common unit of measurement for drawing figures.

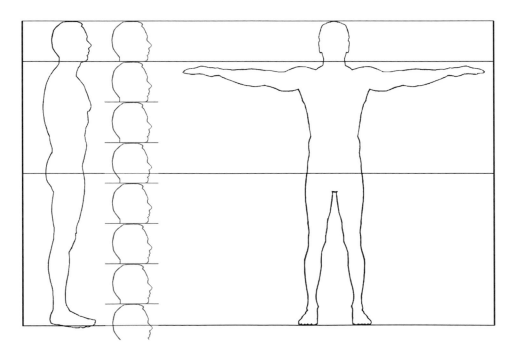

Here you can see the female figure with the same charts. Notice that she is also about seven and a half heads high, even though she is most likely shorter than the male figure. This is because a person's head is usually proportional to his or her body.

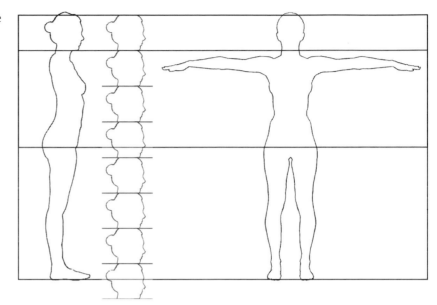

There are a number of major differences between the male and female figures. Male figures tend to be thicker and heavier in the arms and shoulders, while female figures are usually heavier in the hip area and upper legs. The male figure is widest at the shoulders, as shown here.

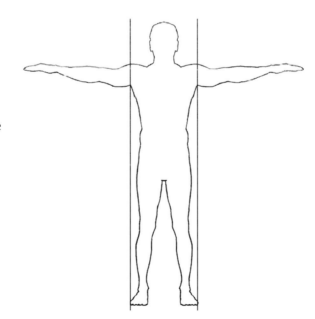

The female figure is wider at the hips.

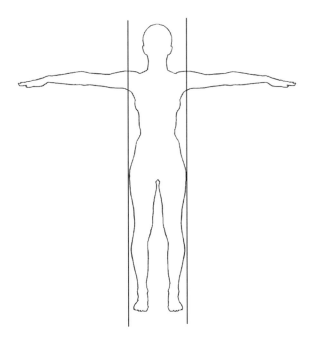

The male figure tends to be thicker through the torso, particularly the upper torso and chest. The female chest is distinguishable by being narrower and has the addition of the female breasts. The male's bone and muscle structure is heavier than the female's. Everything about the female figure tends to be more delicate than the male figure. The bones are smaller and the features are more rounded on a female than on a male. Here you can see the two figures overlaid on each other.

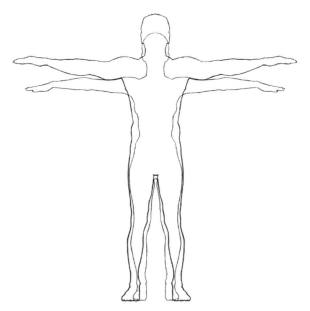

The male figure's shoulders are about three heads wide, while the female's are only about two.

Beginning artists often miss a key balance point for drawing standing figures. When standing from the side, the body of both the male and female figure leans forward, as shown in these two images.

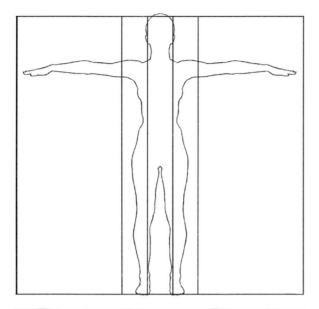

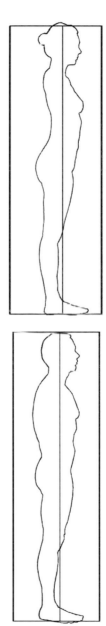

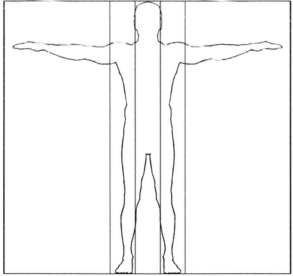

Another interesting fact about both the male and female figures is that the distance from fingertip to fingertip is equal to the height of the figure, as shown in these images.

These are only a few basic elements of a very complex biological system. To understand it fully, you will need to spend some serious time learning anatomy. When I was learning the figure, I spent a lot of time studying the individual bones and muscles to learn how they work in the body.

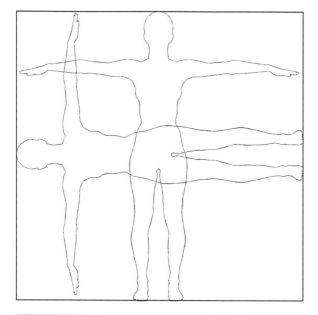

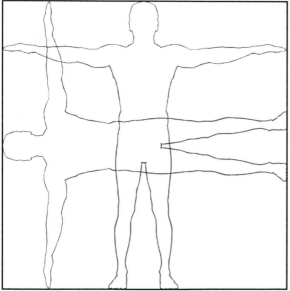

Drawing the Figure

Drawing the figure is similar to drawing the head, except whereas the head is pretty much a ball with features added, the figure is a flexible form with extreme movement possibilities. When drawing the figure, the artist needs to interpret the dynamics of the range of motion within the character's pose. The artist also needs to take into account things such as balance, distribution of weight, action, and proportions. This all sounds complex, but it can be simplified in a similar way to when you were drawing the head. If you can draw a stick figure, you can begin to draw characters.

Here you see a typical stick figure. Next to him is the figure you will use to create characters.

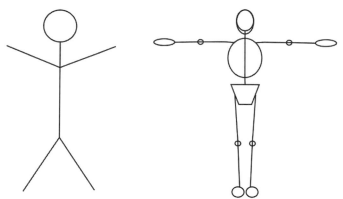

The main difference for the new stick figure is that it includes an oval for the ribcage and a trapezoid for the hips. It is also proportionally correct for the average human character. Here you can see the stick figure from the back, front, and side views.

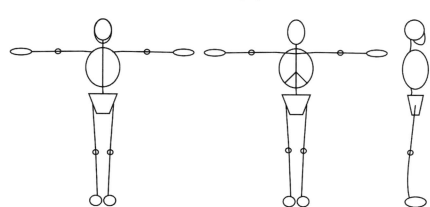

In this image, the stick figure is overlaid on a drawing of the ideal male proportions. Try drawing a few stick figures to get the proportions right.

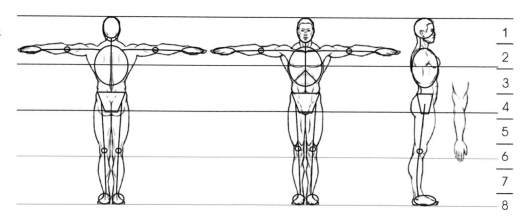

1
2
3
4
5
6
7
8

Once you get the basics of the stick figure down, you can start moving him around to almost any pose, like the one shown here. The stick figure here is high-stepping and appears to be moving in an animated way.

Creating the stick figure in action begins with a simple line called an *action line*. The action line is the main line of movement for the body. If you can visualize the body moving in space and you can define the line of movement from the head along the spine and then through the legs, you will have the action line. Here you can see the beginning action line for a stick figure.

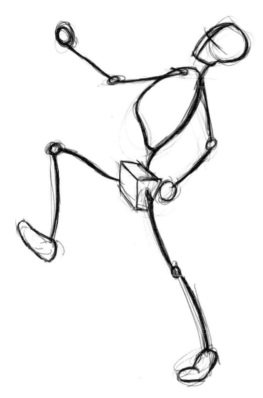

Over the top of the action line, the stick figure is loosely sketched in to indicate the position of the torso and the limbs. Notice how the figure follows the action line in this drawing.

think about where the leg is in space and what you would actually see from your point of view. Drawing the body correctly when part or all of it is rotated toward the viewer is called *foreshortening*.

The action line helps to give the character a feeling of movement. Notice that even though the character's right leg is lifted and pointing toward us, it can still be drawn with the stick figure. Limbs that are pointing toward the viewer are sometimes tricky for beginning artists. The key is to draw the stick figure correctly. Look how that part of the character is drawn. To make the figure look correct, you have to

And now you see the completed stick figure in action. This could be a superhero pose for a super-powerful game character. The only thing that remains now is to add some flesh to the sticks, or bones. In this next example, I will show you how to do this.

Adding Detail

Here you can see how the stick figure was used to create the foundation for the drawing at the beginning of this section.

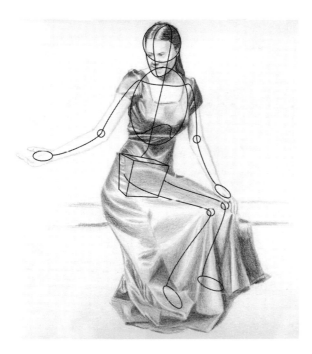

If you have some tracing paper or other paper that is easy to see through, try applying the stick figure to some pictures from a magazine or a fashion catalogue. See whether you can work out how the stick figure is placed inside the body of each person in the pictures.

This is a picture of my grandfather while he was still young. I don't remember grandfather looking like this because when I came along he was much older and was missing one arm. When I found this picture, I just had to create a drawing from it.

1 The very first step is to lightly draw in the stick figure. This will give you a guide for working in the more detailed drawing. If you have ever drawn a person only to find there wasn't enough room for his feet because you ran out of paper, you will find that you can eliminate that problem by drawing the stick figure first. During this stage you want to capture the feeling of the figure and also define all of the major proportions.

2 The next stage is blocking in the figure. Here is where you use the stick figure to guide the placement of the detail.

3 I always tend to start with the head because that seems to be the usual focal point of a figure drawing. I also start to define the light-to-dark contrast of the figure.

4 The next important area of the drawing is the dog, so that is the next thing I render. Notice that I am also working my way from the top of the drawing downward. This helps keep the lower portions of the drawing from getting smudged.

5 Next I work on the coat and shirt. He is wearing a plaid shirt, so I indicate that lightly, as shown here.

6 Here you can see the drawing as it nears completion. There are only a few minor things yet to finish.

7 Once the entire drawing is rendered, I take some time to adjust areas of value so they look correct. I noticed that the area below his arm was too light, so I darkened that area. I also cleaned up any stray lines around the figure. Here you can see the finished drawing.

Once you get the hang of drawing the stick figure, you will be able to construct figures doing anything you imagine. Use the framework to draw some full figure drawings, like the one of the woman at the beginning of this section.

I hope this chapter has helped to reduce your fear of drawing people and has given you a lot of good information about how to see and draw people. Drawing people is fun. Keep practicing, and you will start to see some of the possibilities.

Freeing the Spirit

So far in this book we have spent a lot of time covering how to draw what you see. In this last chapter, I want to explore drawing from imagination—in other words, drawing from the artist's vision.

If all an artist did was draw accurate reproductions of life, the artist would be worth little more than a camera. For art to really be meaningful, it has to have more to it than just a faithful reproduction. It needs to convey the artist's vision.

At the beginning of this book, I defined artistic vision as a way to see the world. Now we need to define it also as a way of expression. It is a way of putting on paper something that is a combination of what you see and observe and your own feelings or thoughts.

Developing Creativity

I often hear people say, "I can't be an artist because I am just not very creative." No matter how true that statement might be at the moment, it doesn't have to be that way in the future. Over the years as I have worked as an artist, I have found that creativity is something that can be learned. You can improve your creative thought. In fact, if you really want to, you can become a creative powerhouse. Drawing can be your path to that new creative you.

Creative Process

In my years as an artist, I have learned a lot about creativity. One thing that became evident to me early on is that there is a process I go through when I am working out a creative problem. I call it the creative process, and it has five steps.

- ▶ **Need**
- ▶ **Learn**
- ▶ **Examine**
- ▶ **Connect**
- ▶ **Results**

Once I learned how this creative process worked, I was able to improve and direct my creative efforts. If I wanted to find a creative solution to a problem I just went through the process, and in most cases I was able to get results.

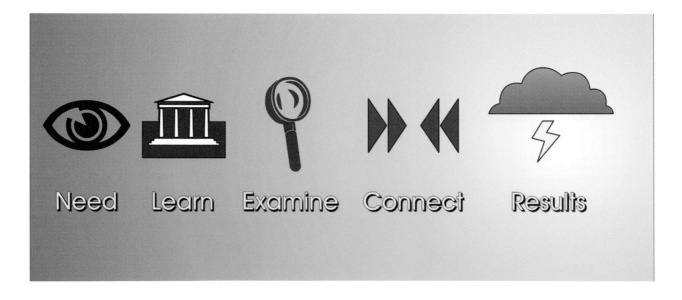

Need   Learn   Examine   Connect   Results

Need

Although I have had creative bursts of thought about things that had nothing to do with anything I was working on, they have been rare. Instead, the majority of my most creative ideas have come from a need of some kind. For example, I might have an assignment to create a character design for a video game. My client comes to me with a vague idea of who the character is and what the character does in the game, but has no idea of what the character should look like. In this case the client establishes the need.

In this example the need is coming from an external party. For the professional artist, this is often the case. For the beginning artist, the need generally comes from within. Maybe the need is something as simple as a need to escape from the world or a need for fulfillment. Another common need for the beginner is the desire to improve in drawing skill.

It is difficult to be creative in a vacuum. Usually creative thought needs a focus. In other words, if you are trying to think of something, it helps to have something to think about, such as drawing funny characters or creating a detailed portrait.

Start with things that are close to you or things you know a lot about. Maybe you have a big family. You could try drawing your family members doing different activities. Maybe you have a favorite pet or a love of animals. You could try drawing animals. Maybe your passion is sports. Try drawing sports characters. If the subject is something you are already familiar with and see on a daily basis, you will already know a lot about it. You might be amazed at how much more you will learn about the subject once you start drawing it.

Learn

Without information there is little chance there will be any creativity. In fact, there is little chance that anything will happen at all. Let me give you an example. Suppose there is local art show coming up and you need to submit a great picture for the competition. What do you draw?

Good question, isn't it? What will be your next masterpiece? Maybe you need some way to narrow down the choices.

Artists often struggle with what is called the *white canvas syndrome*. Because we are drawing instead of painting, we can call it the *white paper syndrome*. Often the most intimidating thing an artist can encounter in the studio is a completely blank white sheet of paper that needs to have a drawing on it. The more important the drawing, the more intimidating the paper can become.

Let's look at another example. Suppose I asked you to creatively capture the personality of a fictional character from a specific book. Would you be able to draw an accurate picture of the character from that assignment? You probably wouldn't be able to draw much because there just wasn't enough information. Even if you did try to come up with some kind of drawing, there is very little chance that you could capture the personality of someone if you have no information about his or her persona. At this point you don't even know whether the character is male or female.

Some people think that withholding information will cause a person to be more creative, but I disagree. In my experience, information feeds creativity. Let's try the assignment once again, this time with more detailed information.

Creatively capture the personality of the fictional character Lisa from the book *Lisa Learns to Ride*. The book is a fictional tale of a young girl from New York who spends the summer with her grandfather on a ranch in Idaho. Lisa is a shy, quiet girl who has never been around animals. When she arrives in Idaho, her grandfather entrusts to her the care of a young captured mustang recently brought in from the mountains. Over the course of the book, Lisa and the horse overcome their fear of each other and become loving riding companions, changing both of their lives forever.

Okay, was that drawing assignment better? As you read the assignment, were you imagining some pictures of a young girl and a horse with the backdrop of the mountains of Idaho? You still don't have all of the information, but you have a start. You know that Lisa is a shy girl from New York City. You know the book takes place on a ranch in Idaho. You know the book is about horses, particularly a young mustang. Is that enough? Maybe it is, but what if you don't know anything about mustangs or ranches in Idaho? You still don't know what Lisa looks like, other than that she is a young girl.

You see, to truly be creative with a picture, you have to be able to see the picture clearly in your mind. It is difficult to visualize something that you are unfamiliar with. When approaching a creative problem, try to immerse yourself in information about the subject. In this particular example, you could start with the book. Reading the book will give you some ideas about the girl and her personality. Next, research the location. Because the book is fictional, there is no actual location. Research as much information on ranches in Idaho as you can find.

The next page shows some pictures my grandmother took when she lived on a farm in northern Idaho. These are the types of pictures you might want to look for to help give you an idea of ranch life.

You might want to research wild horses (mustangs) and ranch clothing styles. The idea of the research is to get a clearer idea of the subject and the many elements that could be used in the creation of the drawing.

Now, this might seem like a lot of work for a drawing. You are right; it is a lot of work, but hopefully it is fun work. If you are really interested in being creative with your drawings or anything else, you have to put some effort into it.

Many rewards come to artists because of the things they learn from their work. I have had the opportunity to learn about many subjects, from medieval weaponry to modern fighter aircraft, and from ancient Egyptian costumes to the latest fashion trends.

Examine

After you have taken the time to gather information about your picture, it is time to start examining the information. Remember how in Chapter 7 the head was isolated into individual features? Each feature was examined in detail to help you learn how to draw it. That is a little like this next step in the creative process. Now it is time to examine and draw different elements that you want to put together in your picture.

Now the sketchbook will become your best friend. Rather than simply throwing a picture together or sitting and designing a final drawing, spend some time just drawing things that relate to the subject. Here you can see a page of sketches. There are different pictures of girls and horses, all loosely related to the subject.

There might be nothing in the sketches that makes its way into the final drawing, but in drawing different elements you do a couple of important things. First, you let your mind relax and think about the problem without any pressure. Second, you learn a lot about the specific issues surrounding the drawing of the subject. As these two things happen, confidence is increased and creativity begins to come to the surface.

While drawing can often be relaxing, drawing a final picture for a client, art show, or any other situation where the work will be on display can at times be stressful. Stress is often the counter to creativity. A good way to take away the pressure is to pull out the sketchbook and do some low-pressure sketches.

Hint

A sketchbook should be a lot like a journal. It should be a private repository of your thoughts and ideas in picture form. I rarely show my sketchbook to anyone. It is a private book where I can draw with no pressure. I don't have to worry about whether my drawings are good or bad. I don't have to stress over composition or focal points. I just draw what I want and enjoy the pure pleasure of drawing, knowing that I'm the only one who will see my drawings.

I think that in life we need private places where our imagination can work without the pressure of outside criticism. For me, that private place is my sketchbook. It isn't that I don't enjoy the pressure of creating a masterpiece; it is just that I need times when there is no pressure to gain greater freedom over my art.

In my sketchbook, I can experiment with shapes and forms. I can also investigate different aspects of drawing. More importantly, I can do a bad drawing and not have to worry about it ever being judged by anyone except myself.

Sketches are different than drawings. A sketch can be as detailed as a finished drawing, but it does not have the planning that a finished drawing has. A sketch does not need to be composed or have boundaries. It does not need focal points or paths. Sketches are drawing experiments. Sometimes sketches can be great works of art, but the nice thing is that they never have to be.

As you sketch the different aspects of your subject, there will be an additional learning process that takes place. You will learn more about your subject. You will learn how it absorbs and disperses light. You will gain insight into its structure. You will also become more comfortable drawing it. It is a lot easier to draw something that you know well than to draw something that is unfamiliar.

Examining the subject through sketching also sparks ideas for compositions and invokes thoughts about the elements that might be included in the final picture.

Connect

Connect means to put things together. In this stage of the creative process, you need to start assembling the drawing elements of your picture. This is where you start to connect one element of the picture with another element of the picture until you have a finished composition and you're ready to start drawing.

Connections are the threads of creativity. Most creative thought centers around our life experiences. These experiences are organized and sorted in our minds so that we can make sense of our past. Often creativity comes to us when we pull what seem to be unrelated events or experiences close enough together that we can build connections between them. I often think of this thought process as like weaving a tapestry, where each thread is an individual thought. Each thought is connected to an experience. By

pulling seemingly unrelated threads together, new designs will form on the tapestry. Some of the designs will be awful, but others will be good. For example, in this image the knight is not riding a horse, but rather a giant chicken. These two elements are not normally thought of together, but combining them creates an interesting picture.

The connections don't always have to be odd, but odd connections are fun once in a while. Let's try a little experiment and see how you do with connections. In this exercise, there are eight nouns and four boxes. Connect any two words, and then draw a picture that contains both of those items. Try to be creative and make the connection different than what you might normally see. For example, in choosing Skateboard and Tree, you might place the skateboard in the tree, indicating a major crash.

Another more common way to connect things for a picture is to organize elements. This is very similar to the composition principles discussed in Chapter 6. It is a matter of taking all of the thought and drawings that you have worked on and sorting those elements that you want to include in the picture. The best way to do this is to create very small thumbnail sketches experimenting with different compositions. These thumbnail pictures should be so small that you can't draw any detail, just the major elements. Here you can see several small thumbnail pictures used in creating a drawing for the example assignment of creating a picture of a character from a book.

Tree   Car

Pencil   Television

Plant   Phone

Person   Skateboard

The advantage of drawing very small thumbnail sketches is that you can draw a number of them in a relatively short amount of time. This allows you to explore major pictorial elements quickly, without a lot invested in each one.

You should give yourself a little time when doing thumbnails so that you push yourself with your designs. Often beginning artists only explore a few ideas before they settle on a composition for a picture. Instead, set a number of thumbnails, such as 20 or 30, and draw until you have that many thumbnails.

When you are finished drawing, pick the one that you like most and move on to setting up your final drawing.

Results

This last step is not so much a creative step as it is an execution of the creative steps taken earlier. In other words, it is evidence of creativity. Yes, now you can finally start drawing your final picture.

Let's go back to the assignment in the example. I decided on three elements for my picture: the girl, the mustang, and the Idaho landscape.

1 First I select one of the thumbnails and work up a composition for the picture using geometric lines. These lines will guide the placement of elements in the scene.

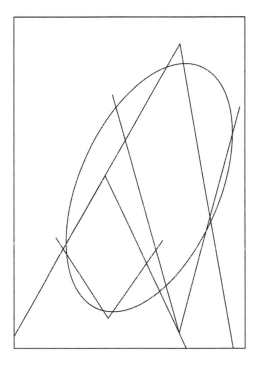

2 I next pull out a clean sheet of drawing paper and lightly sketch in the picture in outline form, as shown here. I place the girl in the lower part of the picture with her head down to indicate that she is shy. The horse is behind the girl, indicating that it is a secondary element, but it is much larger than the girl to show that it is very important. The horse is also very close to the girl to emphasize the bond between it and the girl. Behind the horse are the low, pine-covered hills of Idaho.

Here you can see the geometric composition overlaying the blocked-in drawing.

3 Because the girl is the most important part of the picture, I start rendering her first. I want to establish the form of her head in relation to her shoulders and the horse behind her.

4 Because I want the girl to stand out, I lay in the darkest darks next to the white of her skin, as shown here. The darks and lights will have their strongest contrast in the area around the girl's head and the horse's mouth.

5 Next I draw the horse behind the girl. I reduce the amount of overall contrast with distance from the girl's head. Thus, the horse's ears, which should have dark shadows, are lighter than the area near its mouth, as shown here.

6 The last elements to go into the picture are the background hills and trees. These are drawn in as background elements, so the contrast is lower than in the main area at the front of the picture.

So that is the creative process. Try using it to do your own drawing based on the assignment shown in this example. You don't have to use the creative process only for drawing pictures. The only thing that really changes when using the creative process for other projects is the Results stage. Instead of a drawing, your project might be designing your living room. The results will be the living room instead of a drawing. You can, of course, draw your living room design, but the result is the end accomplishment, not the drawing.

Exaggeration

Exaggeration is a great tool for freeing creativity and expression. Take, for example, exaggerating something in size in a drawing. The exaggerated element has more emphasis. In this image the character has exaggerated arms and shoulders compared to his head. This gives him a feeling of massiveness.

By exaggerating certain attributes of a character, you can make the character cute, goofy, menacing, or possessing almost any other attribute you might think of. Many cartoon characters are created with exaggerated features to emphasize different aspects of the character. Editorial cartoons are famous for exaggerating features of prominent personalities.

When you are creating an exaggerated drawing, the process is still pretty much the same as creating a realistic drawing, except that the reference is interpreted rather than copied. Sometimes no reference is used at all, and the drawing is purely the imagination of the artist. For example, suppose you want to create a Granny character. You start by using a guide, just like you did for drawing a portrait, except that the guide is adapted to the overall shape of the character's head. Here is an example of a drawing guide for a cartoon head.

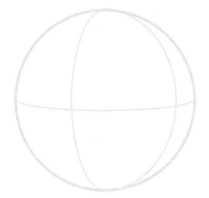

Using the guide, lightly draw in the main features of the head, as shown here. Notice how the nose and chin are exaggerated on the head.

Once you have the features placed where they belong, you can finish drawing in the cartoon head, as shown here.

Exaggeration is used in many other types of art. For example, this character design for a pirate girl is for a video game. Can you spot the exaggeration used in her design?

Let me give you some help. Look at the pirate character's design next to the proportions for a normal human character. Notice the extreme difference in the length of the pirate girl's legs. They are much longer than the normal human proportions. This gives the pirate girl a more active, athletic look.

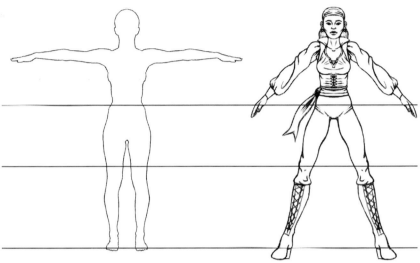

Try drawing some of your own characters, exaggerating different aspects such as the size of the character's eyes in proportion to the head or the size of the head in proportion to the body. Use your imagination and see what you come up with.

Freeing the Spirit

The artist's imagination is at the heart of creativity. You release your imagination through your drawings, giving expression to your own artistic vision. Your drawings are the evidence of your own unique artistic vision.

In this book we have covered a number of basic drawing concepts. I want to encourage you to use the knowledge you have gained to create your own unique artistic vision of your world. Take time to draw every day. Give expression to your ideas and your thoughts.

I hope you can see from the material in this book why everyone should draw. Learning to draw will enrich and improve anyone's life because it teaches people to see and to express, two of the most fundamental aspects of life.

Index

C

M

N

O